CREATIVE CHICKEN

Food Editor: Rachel Blackmore
Subeditor: Ella Martin
Editorial Coordinator: Margaret Kelly
Editorial Assistant: Sheridan Packer
Recipe Development: Sheryle Eastwood, Carolyn
Fienberg, Joanne Glenn, Lucy Kelly, Anneka Mitchell,
Penelope Peel, Belinda Warn, Loukie Werle
Credits: Recipes pages 98, 106 by Louise Steel; pages 8,
78, 89 by Lesley Mackley; pages 16, 17 by Lorna Rhodes
© Merehurst Limited
Photography: Simon Butcher, Per Ericson, Paul Grater,
Ashley Mackevicius, Harm Mol, Yanto Noerianto,
Andrew Payne, Jon Stewart, Warren Webb
Styling: Wendy Berecry, Belinda Clayton, Carolyn
Fienberg, Anna Philips, Jacqui Hing, Michelle Gorry
Production Manager: Sheridan Carter
Layout: Lulu Dougherty
Design: Frank Pithers
Finished Art: Gavin Murrell, Lulu Dougherty

Published by
Chartwell Books, Inc.
A division of BOOK SALES, INC.
110 Enterprise Avenue
Secaucus, New Jersey 07094

© J.B. Fairfax Press Pty Limited, 1992, 1993
A.C.N. 003 738 430

JBFP 211 US
Creative Chicken
Includes Index
ISBN 1 55521 849 0

Formatted by J.B. Fairfax Press Pty Limited
Printed by Toppan Printing Co, Singapore
PRINTED IN SINGAPORE

CREATIVE
CHICKEN

CHARTWELL
BOOKS, INC.

CONTENTS

SOUPS

Whether it's a clear consommé or a hearty chicken and vegetable, nothing beats homemade chicken soup. This selection of recipes shows you just how versatile chicken soup can be – there's something to suit all tastes.

Curried Chicken Soup

CURRIED CHICKEN SOUP

^{1}/4 cup/^{1}/2 stick/60 g butter
2 onions, chopped
2 cloves garlic, crushed
2 large parsnips, chopped
2 stalks celery, chopped
3 tablespoons all-purpose flour
1 tablespoon curry powder
6 cups/1.5 litres chicken stock
6 oz/185 g fresh or frozen green peas
1 pound/500 g cooked chicken, chopped
1 cup/250 g sour cream
3 tablespoons finely chopped parsley
2 tablespoons chopped fresh dill

1   Melt butter in a large saucepan and cook onions, garlic, parsnips and celery over a low heat for 5-6 minutes or until vegetables are just tender. Stir in flour and curry powder and cook for 1 minute longer.

2   Remove pan from heat and gradually blend in stock. Cook, stirring constantly, over a medium heat for 8-10 minutes or until soup boils and thickens. Reduce heat, stir in peas and chicken and cook for 10 minutes longer.

3   Remove pan from heat, whisk in sour cream, then stir in parsley and dill. Cook, stirring frequently, over a low heat for 3-4 minutes or until soup is heated. Serve immediately.

Serves 6

A hearty soup that only requires crusty bread to make it a complete meal.

CREAMY CHICKEN SOUP

1 tablespoon/15 g butter
1 clove garlic, finely chopped
8 cups/2 litres chicken stock
2 pounds/1 kg cooked chicken, finely chopped
2 teaspoons Worcestershire sauce
2 cups/500 mL heavy cream
freshly ground black pepper
4 tablespoons chopped fresh parsley
4 tablespoons snipped fresh chives

1   Melt butter in a large saucepan and cook garlic over a low heat for 2-3 minutes. Add stock, bring to the boil, then reduce heat to simmering, stir in chicken and Worcestershire sauce, and cook for 2-3 minutes.

2   Stir in cream and season to taste with black pepper. Add parsley and chives and cook over a medium heat for 4-5 minutes or until soup is hot.

Serves 8

Cooked chicken is a quick and easy way to make chicken soup. But remember, do not cook the chicken for too long after adding to the soup or it will end up as unpalatable strings.

CHICKEN NOODLE SOUP

A homemade, well-seasoned, clear chicken broth filled with chicken, vegetables and noodles is far superior to most of the packet soups you buy in food shops.

4 cups/1 litre chicken stock
1 carrot, cut into matchsticks
1 leek, thinly sliced
4 oz/125 g cooked chicken, chopped
3 oz/90 g round egg noodles, broken into pieces
freshly ground black pepper
4 sprigs cilantro (fresh coriander)

1   Place stock in a large saucepan and bring to the boil. Add carrot and leek, cover, bring to simmering and simmer for 5 minutes or until carrot is tender.

2   Stir in chicken and noodles and cook for 5-10 minutes or until noodles are tender. Season to taste with black pepper. Serve garnished with cilantro (fresh coriander) sprigs.

Serves 4

Chicken Noodle Soup

Chicken and Avocado Soup

CHICKEN AND AVOCADO SOUP

1 tablespoon/15 g butter
1 onion, finely chopped
1 large potato, diced
3 cups/750 mL chicken stock
10 oz/315 g canned sweet
corn kernels, drained
12 oz/375 g cooked chicken, chopped
freshly ground black pepper
3 tablespoons cream or
evaporated skim milk
1 avocado, peeled, stoned and diced

1   Melt butter in a large sauccpan and cook onion for 2-3 minutes or until soft. Stir in potato and stock, cover, bring to simmering and simmer for 10-15 minutes or until potato is tender.

2   Add sweet corn, chicken and black pepper to taste and cook for 5-6 minutes or until soup is hot. Spoon soup into individual serving bowls. Swirl in cream or milk and top with avocado. Serve immediately.

Serves 4

Chicken and avocados seem to go together like bread and butter, and no more so than in this substantial soup. For a wonderful luncheon, serve the soup with crusty bread and follow with a mixed green salad.

Italian Chicken Soup

ITALIAN CHICKEN SOUP

12 cups/3 litres chicken stock
4 boneless chicken breasts, skinned
1 teaspoon whole black peppercorns
4 bay leaves
1 sprig fresh rosemary
1 onion, chopped
1 red pepper, chopped
2 carrots, chopped
6 oz/185 g short pasta shapes,
such as macaroni
8 oz/250 g cabbage, shredded
2 tablespoons shredded Parmesan cheese

1 Place stock in a large saucepan and bring to the boil. Add chicken breasts, peppercorns, bay leaves and rosemary. Reduce heat, cover and simmer for 20 minutes or until chicken is just cooked.

2 Using a slotted spoon, remove chicken from pan and set aside to drain. Strain stock and return liquid to a clean saucepan. Add onion, red pepper, carrots and pasta to stock, cover, then bring to simmering and simmer for 20 minutes or until pasta is cooked and vegetables are tender.

3 Slice chicken. Stir chicken and cabbage into soup and cook for 5 minutes longer. Just prior to serving, stir in Parmesan cheese.

Serves 6

This clear chicken broth made with fresh chicken and vegetables makes a nutritious and delicious light meal that any weight watcher will love.

10

CREAMY POTATO SOUP

$^{1}/_{3}$ cup/90 g butter
1 onion, chopped
2 cloves garlic, crushed
4 large potatoes, chopped
1 leek, chopped
3 cups/750 mL chicken stock
$^{1}/_{2}$ teaspoon ground nutmeg
1 cup/250 mL heavy cream
freshly ground black pepper
2 tablespoons snipped fresh chives

CROUTONS
2 tablespoons vegetable oil
4 slices thick white bread, cut into
small strips

1   Melt butter in a large saucepan, add onion and garlic and cook, stirring, over a medium heat for 2 minutes. Add potatoes, leek, stock and nutmeg, bring to simmering and cook over a medium heat, stirring occasionally, for 20 minutes or until vegetables are tender.

2   Remove soup from heat and set aside to cool slightly. Place soup in batches in a food processor or blender and process until smooth.

3   Return soup to a clean saucepan, add cream and mix well to combine. Cook over a medium heat, stirring occasionally, for 10 minutes or until heated through. Season to taste with black pepper.

4   To make Croutons, heat oil in a skillet over a medium heat, add bread strips and cook, turning frequently, for 2 minutes or until bread is golden. To serve, ladle soup into bowls, top with Croutons and sprinkle with chives.

Serves 4

A homemade chicken stock makes the difference to this creamy soup (see page 103 for making your own). Remember stock can be made in advance and frozen.

Creamy Potato Soup

CHILI CHICKEN SOUP

3¹/₂ oz/100 g fresh egg noodles
2 tablespoons peanut oil
2 onions, chopped
2 cloves garlic, crushed
1 red chili, finely sliced
1 teaspoon curry paste (vindaloo)
¹/₄ teaspoon ground turmeric
1 tablespoon finely chopped
fresh lemon grass or 1 tablespoon
finely grated lemon rind
4 cups/1 litre coconut milk
1¹/₂ cups/375 mL chicken stock
12 oz/375 g cooked chicken, chopped
3 spinach leaves, finely shredded

1   Cook noodles in a large saucepan of boiling water for 3-4 minutes or until tender. Drain, then rinse noodles under cold running water. Drain again and place in individual bowls.

2   Heat oil in a large saucepan and cook onions for 2-3 minutes or until golden. Stir in garlic, chili, curry paste, turmeric and lemon grass, and cook for 1 minute.

3   Combine coconut milk and chicken stock. Add coconut milk mixture, chicken and spinach to pan. Bring to simmering and simmer for 3-4 minutes. Spoon soup over noodles in bowls and serve immediately.

Serves 6

Coconut milk can be purchased canned, or as a long-life product in cartons, or as a powder to which you add water. These products have a short life once opened and should be used within a day or so.

Chili Chicken Soup

You can make coconut milk using desiccated coconut and water. To make, place 1 pound/500 g flaked coconut in a bowl and pour over 3 cups/750 mL of boiling water. Leave to stand for 30 minutes, then strain, squeezing the coconut to extract as much liquid as possible. This will make a thick coconut milk. The coconut can be used again to make a weaker coconut milk.

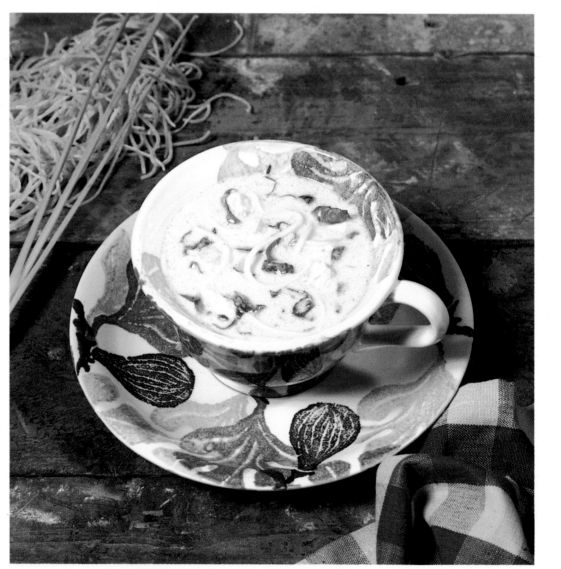

CHICKEN AND CORN SOUP

1 large potato, diced
1 large onion, sliced
6 cups/1.5 litres chicken stock
$^1/_2$ teaspoon chili powder, or
according to taste
8 oz/250 g cooked chicken, chopped
10 oz/315 g canned sweet corn
kernels, drained
2 tablespoons finely chopped
fresh parsley
freshly ground black pepper

1   Place potato, onion, stock and chili powder in a large saucepan, bring to simmering and simmer for 20 minutes or until vegetables are tender.

2   Using a slotted spoon remove vegetables from soup, place in a food processor or blender and process until smooth.

3   Return vegetable purée to stock mixture and mix to combine. Add chicken and sweet corn to soup and cook, over a medium heat for 10 minutes or until heated through. Stir in parsley and season to taste with black pepper.

Serves 6

The puréed vegetables in this soup act as a thickening agent without adding calories.

COMBINATION NOODLE SOUP

2 teaspoons peanut oil
1 onion, finely chopped
1 red pepper, finely chopped
2 x 14 oz/440 g canned chicken
consommé
2 cups/500 mL water
2 boneless chicken breasts, cooked
and thinly sliced
12 large uncooked shrimp, shelled and
deveined
4 oz/125 g rice noodles, cooked
2 oz/60 g oyster mushrooms, sliced
2 oz/60 g canned bamboo shoots, sliced
4 lettuce leaves, shredded
1 tablespoon finely chopped
cilantro (fresh coriander)
freshly ground black pepper

1   Heat oil in a large saucepan, add onion and red pepper and cook, stirring frequently, for 5 minutes or until vegetables are tender.

2   Add consommé and water and bring to the boil. Reduce heat, add chicken, shrimp, noodles, mushrooms and bamboo shoots and simmer for 5 minutes or until shrimp turn pink and are just cooked.

3   Stir in lettuce, cilantro (fresh coriander) and black pepper to taste and serve immediately.

Serves 6

A Chinese-style main meal soup that uses canned consommé as its base is a quick and tasty dish when time is short.

APPETIZERS

*Chicken is especially popular for pre-dinner and cocktail nibbles.
The recipes in this section lend themselves to being served as
small portions for the first course of a formal dinner party or as
finger food for a more informal occasion.*

Mango Chicken Bites

Mango Chicken Bites

1 teaspoon ground cardamom
2 teaspoons ground cumin
¹/2 teaspoon chili powder
1 teaspoon ground ginger
5 boneless chicken breasts,
cut into 1-inch/2.5 cm pieces
2 tablespoons oil

MANGO SAUCE
1 cup/315 g mango chutney
¹/4 cup/60 mL heavy cream
1 tablespoon curry powder

Serves 20 as an hors d'oeuvre

1   Place cardamom, cumin, chili powder and ginger in a bowl and mix to combine. Add chicken and toss to coat with spice mixture. Cover and set aside to marinate at room temperature for 1 hour.

2   Heat oil in a skillet and cook chicken, stirring, over a medium heat for 5 minutes or until cooked. Remove from skillet and drain on paper towels.

3   To make sauce, place chutney, cream and curry powder in a food processor or blender and process to combine. Serve as a dipping sauce with chicken.

As a starter for a formal meal you might like to arrange the chicken pieces on a bed of mixed lettuce leaves with slices of fresh or canned mango. The Mango Sauce could be served in individual pots on the side of each plate.

Oriental Chicken Rolls

¹/2 oz/15 g Chinese dried mushrooms
boiling water
4 spring onions, chopped
2 oz/60 g fresh or frozen peas
freshly ground black pepper
2 boneless chicken breasts, cut into
12 strips, lengthwise
12 sheets rice paper, cut in half
oil for deep-frying

PLUM SAUCE
¹/2 cup/125 mL plum sauce
2 tablespoons water
2 tablespoons finely chopped cucumber

Makes 24 rolls

1   Place mushrooms in a bowl and cover with boiling water. Set aside to soak for 20 minutes or until mushrooms are tender. Drain, remove stalks and chop mushrooms.

2   Place mushrooms, spring onions and peas in a bowl and mix to combine. Season to taste with black pepper.

3   Place a chicken strip and 2 teaspoons mushroom mixture on a corner of each sheet of rice paper, tuck in edges and roll up. Seal, using a little water. Heat oil in a large saucepan and cook 3-4 rolls at a time for 2-3 minutes or until cooked – the rolls will not brown. Remove rolls from oil and drain on paper towels.

4   To make sauce, place plum sauce, water and cucumber in a bowl and mix to combine. Serve with hot rolls.

Chinese dried mushrooms are available from Oriental food shops. They are quite expensive, but keep indefinitely. As their flavor is very strong, only small quantities are used.

DUCK WITH CHERRY SAUCE

2 tablespoons seasoned all-purpose flour
1 teaspoon five spice powder
$1^1/_2$ pounds/750 g boneless duck breasts,
cut into 1-inch/2.5 cm pieces
oil for deep-frying

CHERRY SAUCE
1 tablespoon sugar
12 oz/375 g canned black cherries,
drained
$^1/_3$ cup/90 mL red wine
$^1/_4$ teaspoon mixed spice

Bite-sized pieces of spicy
crisp duck are even more
delicious when dipped in
Cherry Sauce.

Serves 10 as an hors d'oeuvre

1   Place flour and five spice powder in a plastic food bag and shake to combine. Add duck and shake to coat all pieces.

2   Heat oil in a large saucepan and cook duck in batches for 3-4 minutes or until cooked and golden. Drain on paper towels.

3   To make sauce, place sugar, cherries, red wine and mixed spice in a saucepan. Bring to simmering and simmer, uncovered, for 15 minutes. Press cherry mixture through a sieve, return sieved sauce to a clean saucepan and heat gently for 3-4 minutes or until warm. Serve warm as a dipping sauce with hot duck.

CHILI CHICKEN WITH CURRY SAUCE

6 boneless chicken breasts, cut into
1-inch/2.5 cm pieces
$^1/_3$ cup/90 mL vegetable oil
2 teaspoons paprika
$^1/_2$ teaspoon chili powder
oil for deep-frying

CURRY SAUCE
1 tablespoon oil
1 onion, finely chopped
2 teaspoons mild curry powder
1 tablespoon all-purpose flour
$1^1/_4$ cups/315 mL milk
2 tablespoons mango chutney
freshly ground black pepper

Chili-coated chicken pieces
are delicious served with
drinks or as a snack.

Serves 10 as an hors d'oeuvre

1   Place chicken, vegetable oil, paprika and chili powder in a bowl and mix to combine. Cover and set aside to marinate for 1 hour.

2   Heat oil in a large saucepan and cook chicken in batches for 3-4 minutes or until golden and cooked. Drain on paper towels.

3   To make sauce, heat oil in a saucepan and cook onion for 4-5 minutes or until soft. Stir in curry powder and cook for 2 minutes. Add flour and cook, stirring, for 1 minute longer. Gradually stir in milk and bring to the boil, stirring constantly, over a medium heat. Cook for 3-4 minutes or until sauce thickens, then reduce heat and simmer for 5 minutes longer. Stir in chutney and season to taste with black pepper. Serve warm as a dipping sauce with hot chicken.

BACON AND MUSHROOM ROLLS

$^1\!/_4$ cup/$^1\!/_2$ stick/60 g butter
1 onion, finely chopped
6 oz/185 g bacon, chopped
1 pound/500 g chicken livers, trimmed
and chopped
8 oz/250 g mushrooms, chopped
$^1\!/_2$ cup/125 mL chicken stock
2 egg yolks, lightly beaten
$^1\!/_2$ teaspoon mixed dried herbs
freshly ground black pepper
4 sheets phyllo pastry
1 egg white
oil for deep-frying

1   Melt butter in a large skillet and cook onion for 2-3 minutes or until soft. Add bacon and cook for 3-4 minutes longer. Stir in chicken livers and cook, stirring, for 3 minutes or until livers change color. Add mushrooms and cook for 3 minutes longer.

2   Stir in stock, bring to simmering and simmer for 5 minutes or until almost all stock has evaporated. Remove skillet from heat and set aside to cool for 10 minutes.

3   Mix egg yolks, mixed herbs and black pepper to taste into chicken liver mixture. Place chicken liver mixture in a food processor and process to roughly chop. Take care not to make a purée.

4   Cut pastry into twenty-four 6-inch/15 cm squares. Place 2 teaspoons of chicken liver mixture on each pastry square, fold in two edges and roll up like a spring roll. Seal edges with a little egg white.

5   Heat oil in a large saucepan and cook 3-4 rolls at a time for 2-3 minutes or until golden. Remove rolls from oil and drain on paper towels.

Makes 24 rolls

Duck with Cherry Sauce,
Chili Chicken with Curry Sauce,
Bacon and Mushroom Rolls

These crispy rolls filled with chicken livers and mushrooms can be prepared in advance, leaving only the final cooking until just prior to serving. Serve with chili sauce and soy sauce as dipping condiments.

SATAY CHICKEN

One of the most popular of all Asian dishes, these chicken satays will disappear as quickly as you serve them.

4 boneless chicken breasts, cut into ³/4-inch/2 cm cubes

SATAY MARINADE
¹/2 cup/125 mL water
2 tablespoons peanut butter
1 tablespoon honey
1 tablespoon soy sauce
2 tablespoons lemon juice
1 teaspoon chili paste (sambal oelek)
1 teaspoon grated fresh ginger
1 onion, finely chopped

1　To make marinade, place water, peanut butter, honey, soy sauce, lemon juice, chili paste (sambal oelek), ginger and onion in a bowl, and mix to combine.

2　Add chicken to marinade, toss to coat, cover and refrigerate for at least 2 hours or overnight. Remove chicken from marinade and reserve marinade. Thread 2 pieces of chicken onto wooden picks and cook under a preheated broiler for 5 minutes or until cooked.

3　Place reserved marinade in a saucepan and bring to the boil. Reduce heat and simmer for 10 minutes or until marinade reduces and thickens slightly. Serve hot as a dipping sauce with chicken.

Satay Chicken

Makes approximately 20 skewers

SPICY INDIAN CHICKEN

8 boneless chicken breasts, cut into
1-inch/2.5 cm cubes
1 cup/200 g plain yogurt
1 clove garlic, crushed
1 teaspoon grated fresh ginger
$^1/_2$ teaspoon garam masala
$^1/_4$ teaspoon turmeric
$^1/_4$ teaspoon ground cumin
1 tablespoon chopped cilantro (fresh
coriander)
freshly ground black pepper

CUCUMBER CORIANDER DIP
$^1/_2$ cucumber, shredded and drained
1 tablespoon chopped cilantro
(fresh coriander)
$^1/_2$ cup/100 g plain yogurt
$^1/_4$ cup/60 mL heavy cream
freshly ground black pepper

1   Place chicken, yogurt, garlic, ginger, garam masala, turmeric, cumin, cilantro (fresh coriander) and black pepper to taste in a bowl and toss to combine. Cover and refrigerate for at least 4 hours or overnight.

2   Remove chicken from yogurt mixture and place in a single layer on a lightly greased cookie sheet. Cook under a preheated broiler for 5 minutes or until cooked. Spear 1 or 2 pieces of chicken onto wooden picks.

3   To make dip, squeeze excess liquid from cucumber. Place cucumber, cilantro (fresh coriander), yogurt, cream and black pepper to taste in a bowl and mix to combine. Serve with chicken for dipping.

Serves 8

Instead of cutting the chicken breasts into pieces, marinate them whole, then broil and serve with rice and salad for a tasty meal.

SPRING ROLLS

12 spring roll or wonton wrappers, each
5 inches/12.5 cm square
vegetable oil for deep-frying

CHICKEN AND VEGETABLE
FILLING
4 oz/125 g ground chicken
1 oz/30 g bean sprouts
$^1/_4$ small cabbage, chopped
2 spring onions, chopped
1 tablespoon cornstarch
1 tablespoon soy sauce
1 teaspoon sesame oil

1　To make filling, place chicken, bean sprouts, cabbage, spring onions, cornstarch, soy sauce and sesame oil in a bowl and mix to combine.

2　Place a tablespoon of filling in the centre of each wrapper, fold one corner over filling, then tuck in the sides and roll up, sealing with water.

3　Heat vegetable oil in a large saucepan until a cube of bread browns in 50 seconds and cook a few Spring Rolls at a time for 3-4 minutes or until golden. Drain on paper towels and serve immediately.

Spring Rolls

Makes 12

CHICKEN AND LEEK ROLLS

12 spinach lasagne sheets
2 tablespoons grated fresh
Parmesan cheese

CHICKEN AND LEEK FILLING
2 teaspoons vegetable oil
3 leeks, finely sliced
3 boneless chicken breasts, cut into
thin strips
$^1/_2$ cup/125 mL chicken stock
3 teaspoons cornstarch blended with
2 tablespoons water
1 teaspoon French mustard
2 teaspoons chopped fresh basil
freshly ground black pepper

1   Cook lasagne sheets in boiling water in a large saucepan until tender. Drain, set aside and keep warm.

2   To make filling, heat oil in a large skillet and cook leeks and chicken, stirring, for 4-5 minutes or until chicken is brown. Stir in stock, cornstarch mixture, mustard and basil and cook, stirring, for 2 minutes longer. Season to taste with black pepper.

3   Place spoonfuls of filling on lasagne sheets, roll up, top with Parmesan cheese and serve immediately.

Serves 6

Chicken and Leek Rolls

MAIN MEALS

*Broiled, casseroled, fried, baked or roasted,
chicken is a family favorite. Cooks love it because it is
quick and easy to prepare, can be unadorned or dressed up and
combines with many different flavors. These recipes for all
kinds of birds are sure to give you many new ideas.*

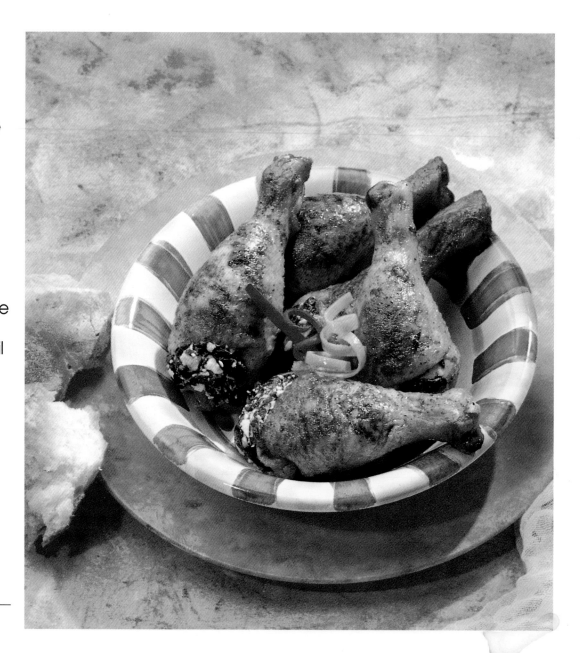

FETA DRUMSTICKS

2 tablespoons/30 g butter
1 clove garlic, crushed
1 bunch English spinach, finely shredded
2 slices ham, finely chopped
4 oz/125 g feta cheese, broken into small pieces
1 teaspoon ground coriander
3 teaspoons ground nutmeg
freshly ground black pepper
12 chicken drumsticks
2 tablespoons olive oil

Serves 6

1   Melt butter in a skillet and cook garlic over a medium heat for 1 minute. Stir in half the spinach and cook for 3-4 minutes or until spinach is wilted. Remove cooked spinach from skillet and set aside. Cook remaining spinach in the same way.

2   Place spinach, ham, feta cheese, coriander, 1 teaspoon nutmeg and black pepper to taste in a bowl and mix to combine. Ease skin carefully away from a drumstick to form a pocket. Place a spoonful of spinach mixture in pocket and pull skin over. Repeat with remaining spinach mixture and drumsticks. Brush drumsticks with oil, sprinkle with remaining nutmeg and place in a baking dish. Bake for 30 minutes or until drumsticks are cooked through.

Oven temperature 350°F, 180°C

These drumsticks are just as good cold or hot. Any leftovers are sure to be popular in packed lunches. If cooked the day before, they are perfect picnic fare.

COCONUT CURRY

1 tablespoon oil
4 boneless chicken breasts, skin removed and halved
2 onions, cut into eighths
2 cloves garlic, chopped
2 tablespoons curry paste
1½ cups/375 mL water
3 potatoes, cut into cubes
3 carrots, sliced
2 stalks fresh lemon grass, bruised, or
1 teaspoon finely grated lemon rind
1 tablespoon cornstarch
½ cup/125 mL coconut milk

Feta Drumsticks

Serves 4

1   Heat oil in a large saucepan and cook chicken for 3-4 minutes or until brown on both sides. Remove chicken from pan and set aside. Add onions and garlic to pan and cook over a medium heat for 4-5 minutes or until onions are soft. Stir in curry paste and cook for 1 minute longer.

2   Return chicken to pan and stir in water, potatoes, carrots and lemon grass or lemon rind. Bring to the boil, then reduce heat, cover and simmer for 30 minutes or until chicken and vegetables are tender.

3   Whisk cornstarch into coconut milk. Stir coconut milk mixture into chicken and cook, stirring, over a medium heat for 4-5 minutes or until curry boils and thickens. Cook for 3 minutes longer. Just prior to serving, remove lemon grass.

If commercially made coconut milk is unavailable, you can make it using desiccated coconut and water. To make coconut milk, place 1 pound/500 g flaked coconut in a bowl and pour over 3 cups/750 mL of boiling water. Leave to stand for 30 minutes, then strain, squeezing the coconut to extract as much liquid as possible. This will make a thick coconut milk. The coconut can be used again to make a weaker coconut milk.

RICE-FILLED CHICKEN

Oven temperature
350°F, 180°C

To test when a bird is cooked, place a skewer into the thickest part of the thigh and when the skewer is removed the juices should run clear. If the juices are tinged pink, return bird to the oven and cook for 15 minutes longer, then test again. On completion of cooking, allow whole birds to stand in a warm place for 10-20 minutes before carving. This tenderizes the meat by allowing the juices to settle into the flesh.

1 x 3 pound/1.5 kg chicken, cleaned
4 slices bacon, chopped
4 spring onions, chopped
2 teaspoons curry powder
^{3}/4 cup/170 g long-grain rice, cooked
1 cup/60 g bread crumbs, made from stale bread
1 tablespoon olive oil

MUSHROOM SAUCE
2 tablespoons/30 g butter
1 onion, chopped
1 green pepper, chopped
4 oz/125 g mushrooms, sliced
14 oz/440 g canned tomatoes, undrained and mashed
2 tablespoons tomato paste (purée)
3 tablespoons red wine
1 tablespoon sugar
^{1}/2 cup/125 mL water
freshly ground black pepper

1   Using paper towels, pat chicken dry inside and out. Cook bacon, spring onions and curry powder in a skillet over a medium heat for 4-5 minutes or until bacon is crisp. Remove skillet from heat and stir in rice and bread crumbs.

2   Fill cavity of chicken with rice mixture and secure opening with metal or bamboo skewers. Tuck wings under body of chicken and tie legs together. Place bird breast side up in a baking dish. Brush with oil and bake, basting frequently with pan juices, for 1^1/2 hours or until bird is cooked.

3   To make sauce, melt butter in a saucepan and cook onion, green pepper and mushrooms for 2-3 minutes. Stir in tomatoes, tomato paste (purée), wine, sugar, water and black pepper to taste. Cook, stirring constantly, over a medium heat for 10-15 minutes or until sauce is reduced by a quarter. Serve sauce with chicken.

Serves 4

CHICKEN WITH CORN

Oven temperature
350°F, 180°C

Serve this rich cumin-flavoured chicken and corn on a bed of boiled rice and accompany with a green vegetable such as beans, asparagus or spinach.

1 tablespoon olive oil
2 onions, chopped
2 teaspoons ground cumin
4 chicken thighs
4 chicken drumsticks
1 cup/250 mL dry white wine
1 cup/250 mL chicken stock
1 cup/250 mL heavy cream
10 oz/315 g canned sweet corn kernels, drained

1   Heat oil in a large skillet and cook onions and cumin over a medium heat for 4-5 minutes or until onions are soft. Add chicken and cook for 8-10 minutes longer or until brown on all sides. Transfer onions and chicken to a casserole dish.

2   Drain fat from skillet and stir in wine. Bring to the boil, stirring and scraping bits from bottom of skillet. Boil for 4-5 minutes or until reduced by half.

3   Stir stock, cream and corn into wine and cook for 5 minutes longer. Pour wine mixture over chicken, cover and bake for 45-60 minutes or until chicken is cooked.

Serves 4

Rice-filled Chicken

ALMOND CHICKEN ROLLS

4 boneless chicken breasts,
skin removed
vegetable oil for deep-frying

BREAD CRUMB COATING
2 eggs
$^1/_3$ cup/90 mL milk
$^1/_2$ cup/60 g seasoned all-purpose flour
2 cups/125 g bread crumbs,
made from stale bread

HERB BUTTER
$^3/_4$ cup/1$^1/_2$ sticks/185 g butter
2 oz/60 g almonds, chopped
2 teaspoons French mustard
1 tablespoon chopped fresh parsley
1 tablespoon snipped fresh chives
freshly ground black pepper

Do not allow the oil to become too hot when cooking these rolls or the coating will brown before the chicken is cooked.

1   To make Herb Butter, soften butter. Place butter, almonds, mustard, parsley, chives and black pepper to taste in a bowl and mix to combine. Divide butter into four portions and shape into 4-inch/ 10 cm long rolls. Wrap rolls in plastic food wrap and refrigerate until firm.

2   Place chicken breasts between two sheets of plastic food wrap and pound, using a rolling pin, to flatten. Take care not to make holes in the breasts or the butter will run out during cooking.

3   Place a butter roll in the centre of each chicken breast. Fold the shorter ends of the breasts into the centre, then roll up to fully encase the butter. Secure with wooden picks.

4   To coat, place eggs and milk in a small bowl and beat to combine. Transfer to a shallow dish. Place flour and bread crumbs on separate plates. Coat chicken rolls with flour, then dip in egg mixture and roll in bread crumbs. Repeat egg and bread crumb steps. Place rolls on a plate, cover with plastic food wrap and refrigerate for 1 hour.

5   Heat oil in a large saucepan and cook chicken rolls for 5-8 minutes or until golden and cooked through.

Serves 4

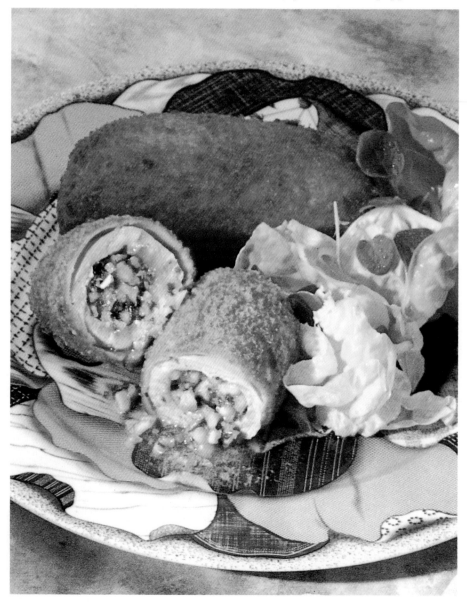

Almond Chicken Rolls

CHICKEN BEAN BAKE

1 slice bacon, chopped
3 pounds/1.5 kg chicken pieces, skin removed
2 onions, chopped
1 clove garlic, crushed
$^1/_2$ cup/125 mL chicken stock
$^1/_3$ cup/90 mL white wine
1 teaspoon dried mixed herbs
1 teaspoon sugar
14 oz/440 g canned tomatoes, undrained and mashed
10 oz/315 g canned lima or butter beans, drained

Chicken Bean Bake   ***Serves 6***

1   Cook bacon in a skillet, over a medium heat for 2-3 minutes or until crisp. Remove bacon from skillet and drain on paper towels.

2   Cook chicken in skillet for 5-8 minutes or until brown on all sides. Remove chicken from skillet and place in a casserole.

3   Add onions and garlic to skillet and cook for 2-3 minutes or until onion is soft. Scatter onion mixture and bacon over chicken pieces.

4   Stir stock, wine, herbs, sugar and tomatoes into skillet and bring to the boil over a medium heat. Cook, stirring occasionally, until mixture reduces and thickens. Stir in beans and pour over chicken. Cover and bake for 45-60 minutes or until chicken is cooked.

Oven temperature
400°F, 200°C

When cooking poultry pieces, remember that the breast – the white meat – cooks more quickly than the legs and thighs – the dark meat. Cooking the leg and thigh portions for 10 minutes before adding the breast portions will give you evenly cooked poultry pieces.

HONEY-GLAZED DUCK

Oven temperature
350°F, 180°C

As a general rule, a 5 pound/ 2.5 kg duck will serve 4 people. Pierce the skin of the duck before cooking and place on a rack set in a baking dish, so that the fat from the duck drains off during cooking.

1 x 5 pound/2.5 kg duck, cleaned
2 onions, halved
5 sprigs fresh parsley

HONEY GLAZE
3 tablespoons honey
1 tablespoon mild mustard
$^1/_4$ cup/60 mL dry sherry

1   To make glaze, place honey and mustard in a small saucepan and cook, stirring, over a medium heat until honey melts. Stir in sherry and bring to the boil, reduce heat and simmer for 2 minutes. Remove pan from heat and set aside.

2   Place onions and parsley in cavity of duck and secure opening with metal or bamboo skewers. Tuck wings under body of duck and tie legs together. Place bird breast side up on a wire rack set in a baking dish. Brush duck with glaze and bake, turning several times, for 1 hour or until duck is cooked.

Honey-glazed Duck

Serves 4

Hens with Olives

HENS WITH OLIVES

2 x 1 pound/500 g Rock Cornish hens
2 tablespoons olive oil
1 teaspoon cracked black pepper
2 teaspoons dried mixed herbs

BLACK OLIVE STUFFING
$^1/_4$ cup/$^1/_2$ stick/60 g butter
4 spring onions, finely chopped
6 slices bacon, finely chopped
3 oz/90 g olives, pitted and chopped
1 cup/60 g bread crumbs,
made from stale bread
1 tablespoon chopped fresh thyme or
1 teaspoon dried thyme

1   To make stuffing, melt butter in a skillet and cook spring onions and bacon over a medium heat for 2 minutes. Remove pan from heat, add olives, bread crumbs and thyme and mix to combine.

2   Fill cavity of each bird with stuffing and secure opening with metal or bamboo skewers. Tuck wings under body of bird, tie legs together and place in a baking dish.

3   Brush birds with oil, sprinkle with black pepper and herbs and bake for 45-60 minutes or until birds are cooked.

Serves 2

Oven temperature
350°F, 180°C

A Rock Cornish hen, is a young chicken weighing 1-2 pounds/500 g-1 kg. It has a delicate flesh and is delicious roasted, broiled, pot-roasted, casseroled or barbecued. Usually one bird is allowed per serving.

BLUEBERRY DUCK

Blueberries are used in this recipe, but any other berry fruit can be used instead.

2 tablespoons vegetable oil
4 duck breasts, with skin
3 tablespoons balsamic or
red wine vinegar
$^1/_4$ teaspoon ground cinnamon
4 tablespoons fresh blueberries
freshly ground black pepper
ZUCCHINI FLOWERS
$^3/_4$ cup/90 g all-purpose flour
1 cup/250 mL water
vegetable oil for deep-frying
12 zucchini flowers

1   Heat oil in a large skillet and cook duck, skin side down, over a low heat for 4-5 minutes or until skin is golden. Turn and cook other side for 3-4 minutes.

2   Add vinegar, cinnamon, blueberries and black pepper to taste. Cover and cook over a low heat for 15 minutes or until duck is tender.

3   To prepare flowers, gradually sift flour into water and mix with a fork until batter is smooth. If necessary, add more water. Pour 1 inch/2.5 cm oil into a skillet and heat until very hot. Dip flowers into batter and cook a few at a time in oil until golden.

4   To serve, arrange duck and flowers on a serving plate and spoon blueberry sauce over duck.

Serves 4

In Italy, zucchini flowers are used in many ways. They can be dipped in batter and fried, or stuffed and then fried or used in risotto. If zucchini flowers are unavailable, do not be put off making this dish – the duck is just as good served with a green vegetable such as asparagus, beans or zucchini.

CHICKEN MARSALA

4 boneless chicken breasts, pounded
3 tablespoons seasoned all-purpose flour
2 tablespoons/30 g butter
2 tablespoons olive oil
$^3/_4$ cup/185 mL dry Marsala
or sherry
$^1/_3$ cup/90 mL chicken stock
2 tablespoons/30 g butter, softened
freshly ground black pepper

1   Coat chicken in flour and shake off excess. Heat butter and oil in a skillet, until butter is foaming. Add chicken and cook for 3 minutes each side.

2   Stir in Marsala or sherry, bring to the boil, reduce heat and simmer for 15 minutes or until chicken is cooked. Remove chicken, set aside and keep warm. Add stock, bring to the boil and boil for 2 minutes. Whisk in softened butter and season to taste with black pepper. To serve, spoon sauce over chicken.

To pound chicken breasts, place between two sheets of plastic food wrap and pound, using a rolling pin, to flatten. Take care not to make holes in the breasts. This method of pounding also prevents the breasts from sticking to the pounding utensil.

Serves 4

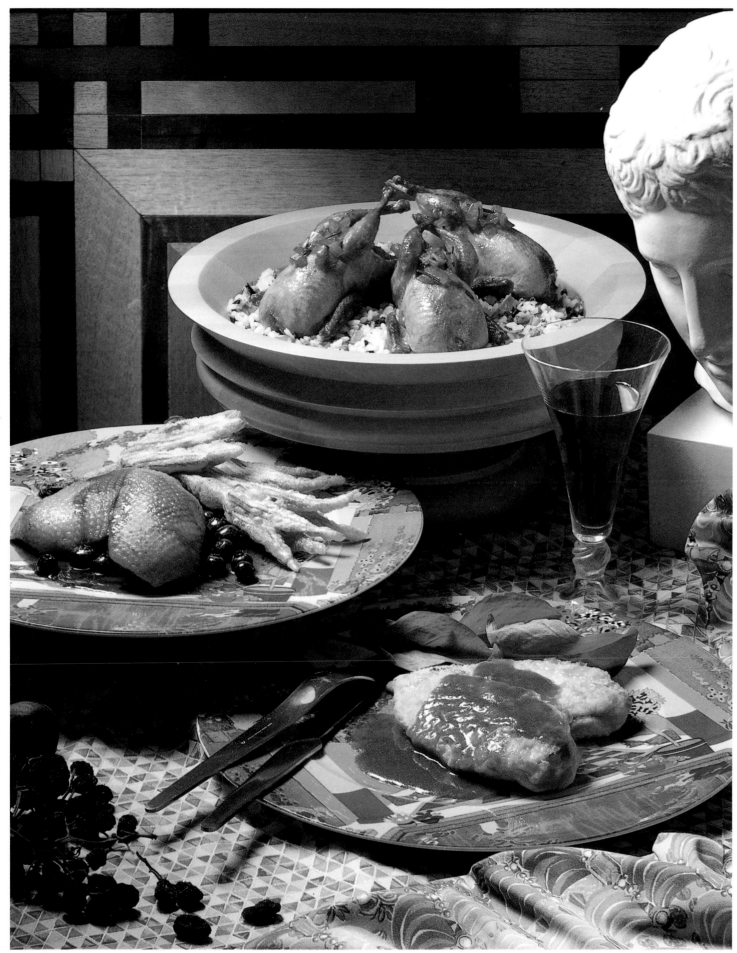

Blueberry Duck,
Chicken Marsala, Quail with Olive Rice

QUAIL WITH OLIVE RICE

1 tablespoon olive oil
2 tablespoons/30 g butter
2 onions, chopped
2 cloves garlic, crushed
8 quails
5 fresh sage leaves
3 teaspoons chopped fresh rosemary or
1 teaspoon dried rosemary
freshly ground black pepper
1¹/₄ cups/315 mL dry sherry

OLIVE RICE
12 oz/375 g rice, cooked
¹/₄ cup/¹/₂ stick/60 g butter, chopped
6 slices mortadella, chopped
3 oz/90 g pitted black olives, chopped
3 tablespoons grated fresh
Parmesan cheese
3 tablespoons chopped fresh basil

1   Heat oil and butter in a skillet and cook onions and garlic over a low heat for 3 minutes or until onions are soft.

2   Add quails to skillet and cook over a high heat until brown on all sides. Add sage, rosemary and black pepper to taste.

3   Stir in sherry, bring to the boil, then reduce heat and simmer for 20 minutes or until quails are cooked.

4   To prepare rice, place rice, butter, mortadella and olives in a saucepan and cook, stirring, over a low heat for 4-5 minutes until butter is melted and mixture is hot. Mix in Parmesan cheese and basil. To serve, divide rice between four serving plates, top with quails and spoon a little of the pan juices over.

Serves 4

How do you eat quail? In your fingers. Just as eating asparagus in your fingers is considered permissible, the same goes for quail. In fact, eating quail any other way is very difficult and you leave behind much of the delicious meat.

ORIENTAL STIR-FRY

2 tablespoons vegetable oil
2 onions, cut into eighths
1 clove garlic, crushed
1 teaspoon grated fresh ginger
8 boneless chicken breasts,
cut into strips
¹/₄ teaspoon ground cumin
¹/₄ teaspoon ground coriander
3 tablespoons oyster sauce
1 teaspoon sesame oil
4 oz/125 g broccoli, cut into florets
4 oz/125 g snow peas, trimmed
1 tablespoon sesame seeds

1   Heat oil in a skillet or wok and stir-fry onions, garlic and ginger for 2-3 minutes or until onions are soft. Remove from skillet and set aside.

2   Add chicken to skillet and stir-fry for 3-4 minutes or until chicken changes color. Place cumin, coriander, oyster sauce and sesame oil in a small bowl, mix to combine, then stir into skillet. Return onion mixture to skillet, add broccoli and snow peas and stir-fry for 3-4 minutes or until broccoli and snow peas are tender. Sprinkle with sesame seeds and serve immediately.

Serves 4

A quick and easy Asian-style dish with a medley of flavors that is sure to be popular. Serve with boiled rice or noodles for a complete meal.

Herb Chutney Chicken

1 x 3 pound/1.5 kg chicken
1/4 cup/1/2 stick/60 g butter, melted
2 cloves garlic, crushed

CHUTNEY STUFFING
2 tablespoons chopped fresh mixed
herbs such as parsley, chives, rosemary,
thyme and oregano
4 oz/125 g grated fresh Parmesan cheese
2 tablespoons fruit chutney
1 egg, lightly beaten
1 cup/60 g dried bread crumbs
1/3 cup/90 g butter, melted

1   To make stuffing, place herbs, Parmesan cheese, chutney, egg, bread crumbs and butter in a bowl and mix to combine. Fill cavity of chicken with stuffing and secure opening with metal or bamboo skewers.

2   Tuck wings under body of chicken and tie legs together. Place bird breast side up in a baking dish. Combine butter and garlic, brush over chicken and bake, turning several times, for 1-1 1/2 hours or until bird is cooked.

Serves 4

Oven temperature
350°F, 180°C

When making stuffing, try doubling the quantity and cooking the remainder in a dish to serve as extra stuffing with the bird. Or use to fill vegetables such as tomatoes and red and green peppers. These vegetables will take 20-30 minutes to cook and can be baked with the chicken.

Herb Chutney Chicken

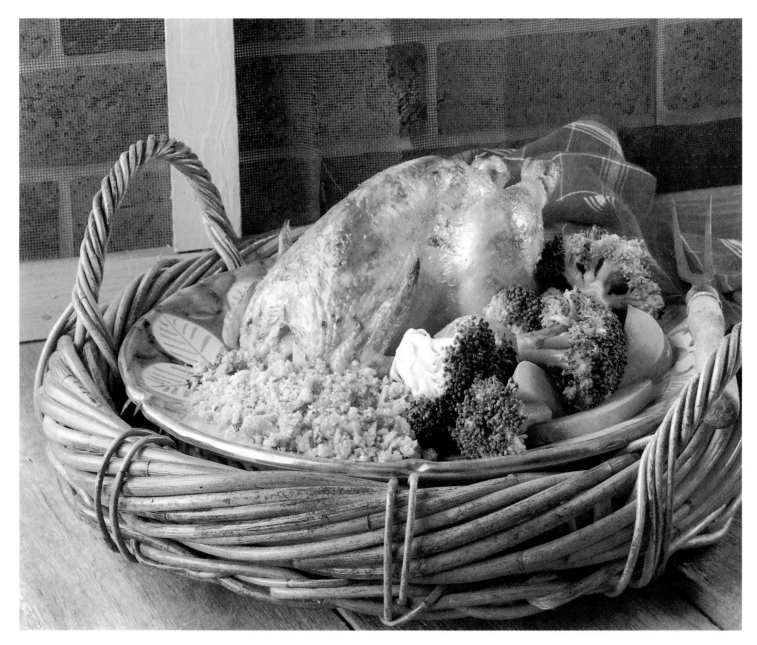

CHICKEN PIE

Oven temperature
350°F, 180°C

A chicken pie with a difference. The corn meal pastry has a deliciously different texture and the filling is like no other you have tasted. For a complete meal, serve with a salad of mixed lettuces, tomatoes and olives tossed in a light vinaigrette dressing.

CORN MEAL PASTRY
1^1/$_2$ cups/185 g all-purpose flour
^{1}/$_3$ cup/60 g corn meal
^{2}/$_3$ cup/155 g butter, cut into pieces
1 egg, lightly beaten
^{1}/$_2$ cup/125 mL water

CHICKEN FILLING
1 tablespoon olive oil
1 pound/500 g frozen spinach, thawed
2 cloves garlic, crushed
1 oz/30 g pine nuts
5 slices prosciutto or ham, chopped
3 chicken breasts, poached and chopped
2 pieces canned red pepper, or ^{1}/$_2$ fresh red pepper cut into strips
3 eggs, lightly beaten
1 cup/250 mL heavy cream
freshly ground black pepper

1   To make pastry, place flour, corn meal and butter in a food processor and process until mixture resembles fine bread crumbs. With machine running, add egg, then water a tablespoon at a time until mixture forms a ball. Turn dough onto a lightly floured surface and knead lightly. Wrap in plastic food wrap and refrigerate for 30 minutes.

2   To make filling, heat oil in a large skillet and cook spinach, garlic, pine nuts and prosciutto or ham over a medium heat for 4-5 minutes or until pine nuts are golden. Transfer spinach mixture to a bowl and set aside to cool completely. Add chicken, red pepper, eggs and cream, and mix to combine.

3   Roll out two-thirds of corn meal dough on a lightly floured surface and line the base and sides of a lightly greased, deep 9-inch/23 cm pie dish. Trim edges using a sharp knife. Spoon filling into pie dish. On a lightly floured surface, roll out remaining pastry large enough to cover pie. Brush edge of pastry with water and cover with pastry top. Press edges together to seal, then trim and make a decorative edge using fingertips. Make two slits in top of pie to allow steam to escape. Bake for 45 minutes or until pastry is golden.

Serves 8

Chicken Pie

CHICKEN ROLL CASSEROLE

6 boneless chicken breasts,
skin removed
3 slices bacon
1 tablespoon chopped fresh parsley
$^1/_4$ cup/$^1/_2$ stick/60 g butter
2 onions, chopped
2 carrots, shredded
8 spinach leaves
freshly ground black pepper
3 potatoes, cooked
$^1/_2$ cup/125 mL water

1   Place chicken breasts between two sheets of plastic food wrap and pound, using a rolling pin, to flatten. Remove rind from bacon and cut each slice in half. Place a piece of bacon on each chicken breast and sprinkle with parsley. Fold the shorter ends of the breasts into the centre, then roll up and secure with wooden picks.

2   Melt half the butter in a large skillet and cook chicken rolls for 8-10 minutes or until brown on all sides. Remove rolls from skillet and set aside.

3   Melt remaining butter in skillet and cook onions and carrots, stirring, for 5 minutes or until onions are soft. Add spinach and cook, stirring, for 2-3 minutes longer or until spinach is wilted. Season to taste with black pepper.

4   Cut potatoes into thick slices and place in the bottom of a casserole dish. Top with vegetable mixture, then chicken rolls. Pour water over, cover and bake for 35-40 minutes or until chicken rolls are cooked.

Serves 6

Oven temperature
350°F, 180°C

Chicken rolls filled with bacon and parsley make a complete meal when teamed with vegetables and cooked in a casserole. Serve with crusty bread rolls or garlic bread.

Chicken Roll Casserole

Honeyed Roast Quail

HONEYED ROAST QUAIL

Oven temperature
350°F, 180°C

Native to the Middle East, the quail is the smallest game bird and is related to the pheasant. It is now reared on farms and considered a gourmet item. Due to the small size of the bird, two are usually considered to be a serving.

4 quails

SOY HONEY GLAZE
1 tablespoon sesame oil
$^1/4$ cup/60 mL soy sauce
$^1/4$ cup/90 g honey
2 tablespoons lemon juice
1 tablespoon sesame seeds

1   To make glaze, place oil, soy sauce, honey, lemon juice and sesame seeds in a small saucepan and cook, stirring, over a medium heat for 10 minutes.

2   Tuck wings under body of each quail and tie legs together. Place breast side up in a baking dish and brush with glaze. Bake, basting several times, for 25 minutes or until birds are cooked.

Serves 2

CHICKEN TERRINE

1 x 3 pound/1.5 kg chicken
8 cups/2 litres water
2 carrots, chopped
2 onions, quartered
2 oz/60 g chopped fresh parsley
1 tablespoon black peppercorns
4 bay leaves
1 tablespoon gelatine
$^1/_4$ cup/60 mL boiling water
2 stalks celery, finely chopped
2 spring onions, finely chopped
1 oz/30 g basil leaves, chopped
8 oz/250 g ham slices, chopped

1   Place chicken, water, carrots, onions, parsley, peppercorns and bay leaves in a large saucepan and bring to the boil. Reduce heat and simmer for 2 hours.

2   Remove chicken from cooking liquid and set aside to cool completely. Strain stock into a bowl and discard vegetables.

3   Strip flesh from chicken, discarding skin and bones. Place chicken flesh in a food processor and process to roughly chop. Take care not to process to a paste.

4   Place strained stock in a clean saucepan, bring to the boil, then reduce heat and simmer, uncovered, until stock is reduced to 3 cups/750 mL. Dissolve gelatine in boiling water then stir into hot stock. Set aside to cool slightly.

5   Place celery, spring onions and basil in a bowl, and mix to combine. Place ham in the base of a loaf pan lined with plastic food wrap, then top with celery mixture and finally with chicken. Pour over stock mixture and press down to evenly distribute stock and to immerse chicken. Cover and refrigerate until set. To serve, turn terrine onto a plate and slice.

Serves 8

Ideal for a garden party or even to take on a picnic, this terrine takes time to prepare, but the delicious flavor makes it worthwhile. One short cut would be to use a barbecued chicken and commercial chicken stock.

Chicken Terrine

AVOCADO STRUDEL

Oven temperature
350°F, 180°C

This recipe is also delicious made with tuna or salmon in place of the chicken. For a lower calorie (kilojoule) version, ricotta cheese can be used instead of cream cheese.

10 sheets phyllo pastry
4 tablespoons vegetable oil
2 tablespoons sesame seeds

CHICKEN AVOCADO FILLING
1 tablespoon oil
1 small onion, chopped
2 teaspoons curry powder
6$^{1}/_{2}$ oz/200 g cream cheese, softened
2 chicken breasts, cooked
and cut into strips
$^{1}/_{2}$ red pepper, sliced
8 button mushrooms, sliced
1 avocado, stoned, peeled and sliced
freshly ground black pepper

1   To make filling, heat oil in a skillet and cook onion and curry powder for 4-5 minutes or until onion is soft. Transfer onion mixture to a bowl, add cream cheese, chicken, red pepper, mushrooms, avocado and black pepper to taste. Mix well to combine.

2   Layer phyllo pastry sheets on top of each other, brushing between layers with oil. Top pastry with chicken mixture and roll up tightly, tucking ends under. Place on a cookie sheet, brush with oil, sprinkle with sesame seeds and bake for 30 minutes or until golden.

Avocado Strudel

Serves 6

CHICKEN BIRYANI

Oven temperature
350°F, 180°C

¹/₃ cup/90 g ghee or butter
3 onions, sliced
3 pounds/1.5 kg chicken pieces
2 teaspoons grated fresh ginger
3 cloves garlic, crushed
¹/₂ teaspoon ground cumin
¹/₂ teaspoon ground cinnamon
¹/₄ teaspoon ground cloves
¹/₄ teaspoon ground cardamom
¹/₄ teaspoon ground nutmeg
¹/₂ teaspoon all-purpose flour
1 cup/250 mL chicken stock
¹/₂ cup/100 g plain yogurt
¹/₂ cup/125 mL heavy cream
2 oz/60 g roasted cashew nuts, chopped

RICE PILAU
¹/₄ cup/¹/₂ stick/60 g ghee or butter
¹/₂ teaspoon ground saffron
¹/₂ teaspoon ground cardamom
1 teaspoon salt
1 cup/220 g basmati rice,
well-washed
4 cups/1 litre chicken stock
2 tablespoons golden raisins

1   Heat ghee or butter in a large skillet and cook onions, stirring, over a medium heat for 5 minutes or until golden. Remove from skillet and set aside. Add chicken to skillet and cook for 3-4 minutes each side or until golden. Remove from skillet and set aside.

2   Add ginger, garlic, cumin, cinnamon, cloves, cardamom, nutmeg and flour to skillet and cook, stirring, for 1-2 minutes. Add stock, yogurt and cream, stirring to lift sediment from bottom of skillet. Return chicken and half the onion mixture to skillet, cover and simmer for 15-20 minutes or until chicken is just cooked. Remove skillet from heat and stand, covered, for 15 minutes.

3   To make pilau, melt ghee or butter in a large saucepan and cook saffron, cardamom, salt and rice, stirring constantly, for 1-2 minutes. Add stock and bring to the boil. Stir in golden raisins, reduce heat and simmer for 10-15 minutes or until most of the stock is absorbed and rice is cooked. Cover and set aside to stand for 10 minutes.

4   Place rice on a large ovenproof serving platter, top with chicken pieces and spoon sauce over. Sprinkle with remaining onions and cashew nuts, cover and bake for 20 minutes.

Serves 4

The Great Moguls (Muslim emperors of India between 1526 and 1857) served biryani at lavish feasts on plates so large that two people were required to carry them.

Chicken Biryani

CHICKEN POT PIE

Oven temperature
400°F, 200°C

A delicious herb topping is an imaginative alternative to potatoes in this cobbler-style recipe. Serve with a green vegetable, such as beans, spinach or cabbage, for a complete meal.

$^{1}/_{4}$ cup/$^{1}/_{2}$ stick/60 g butter
1 large onion, chopped
4 chicken breasts,
cut into $^{3}/_{4}$-inch/2 cm cubes
2 potatoes, cut into $^{1}/_{2}$-inch/1 cm cubes
2 large carrots, cut into
$^{1}/_{2}$-inch/1 cm cubes
$^{1}/_{4}$ cup/30 g all-purpose flour
1 cup/250 mL dry white wine
3 cups/750 mL chicken stock
1 cup/250 mL heavy cream
2 tablespoons tomato paste (purée)

HERBED BISCUIT TOPPING
2 cups/250 g self-raising
flour, sifted
1 teaspoon dried mixed herbs
1 oz/30 g grated fresh Parmesan cheese
2 tablespoons/30 g butter, chopped
1 cup/250 mL milk

1   Melt butter in a large skillet and cook onion, stirring, over a medium heat for 3-4 minutes or until onion is soft. Add chicken and cook, stirring, for 3 minutes longer.

2   Add potatoes and carrots and cook, stirring, for 8-10 minutes. Stir in flour, then wine, stock, cream and tomato paste (purée), and bring to simmering. Simmer for 10 minutes then transfer mixture to a casserole dish.

3   To make topping, place flour, herbs, Parmesan cheese and butter in a food processor and process to combine. With machine running, add milk and process to form a sticky dough. Turn dough onto a lightly floured surface and knead until smooth. Press dough out to $^{3}/_{4}$ inch/2 cm thick and, using a biscuit cutter, cut out rounds and place on top of casserole.

4   Bake for 20-25 minutes or until topping is cooked and golden, and casserole is hot.

Serves 4

Chicken Pot Pie

Herbed Hens

HERBED HENS

4 Rock Cornish hens
4 sprigs fresh thyme
4 slices bacon, rind removed

HERB BUTTER MARINADE
1 tablespoon dried mixed herbs
$^1/_3$ cup/90 g butter, melted
3 tablespoons vegetable oil

Serves 4

1   To make marinade, place herbs, butter and oil in a small bowl and mix to combine.

2   Place a sprig of thyme in cavity of each bird. Tuck wings under birds and tie legs together. Wrap a bacon slice around each bird and secure with a wooden pick. Place birds breast side up in a baking dish, brush with marinade and bake, basting frequently with marinade, for 30-35 minutes or until cooked.

Oven temperature
350°F, 180°C

Delicious served with a tossed salad of mixed lettuce and fresh herbs and crusty wholewheat rolls.

REDCURRANT DUCK

2 tablespoons olive oil
8 duck breasts, with skin
$^1/_4$ cup/60 mL fresh lime
or lemon juice
2 tablespoons honey
$^1/_2$ cup/170 g redcurrant jelly
4 oz/125 g fresh or frozen redcurrants

Pan-cooked duck breasts with a redcurrant sauce make an elegant main course. Serve with asparagus, a sauté of leek strips and new potatoes.

1   Heat oil in a large skillet and cook duck breasts for 7-8 minutes each side or until golden and cooked to your liking. Remove from skillet, set aside and keep warm.

2   Drain fat from skillet and add lime or lemon juice, honey and redcurrant jelly. Bring to the boil over a medium heat, stirring to lift sediment from bottom of skillet. Reduce heat and simmer for 3-4 minutes or until mixture reduces and thickens slightly. Stir in redcurrants and cook, stirring, for 1 minute longer. Serve sauce with duck.

Serves 4

CHICKPEA RAGOUT

$^1/_4$ cup/60 mL olive oil
1 onion, chopped
1 teaspoon ground turmeric
1 x 3 pound/1.5 kg chicken, cut
into 6 pieces
7 oz/220 g chickpeas (garbanzo beans),
soaked overnight, drained
2 cups/500 mL chicken stock
$^1/_4$ cup/60 mL fresh lemon juice
3 cloves garlic, crushed
1 oz/30 g blanched almonds, toasted
1 tablespoon chopped fresh parsley

Chickpeas (garbanzo beans) take 45-60 minutes to cook. The cooking time can vary depending on the quality and age of the chickpeas and their place of origin. This recipe could be made using canned chickpeas. If using canned chickpeas, heat oil in a large skillet and cook onion, turmeric, chicken and garlic, stirring, for 4-5 minutes. Transfer chicken mixture to a saucepan and stir in 2 tablespoons lemon juice, 1 cup/250 mL stock (the remaining lemon juice and stock will not be used in this version of the recipe) and chickpeas. Bring to simmering and simmer for 15-20 minutes or until hot. Just prior to serving, sprinkle with almonds and parsley.

1   Heat oil in a large skillet and cook onion and turmeric, stirring, over a medium heat for 3 minutes or until onion is soft. Add chicken pieces and cook for 4 minutes each side or until golden. Remove chicken pieces from skillet and set aside.

2   Add chickpeas (garbanzo beans), stock, lemon juice and garlic to skillet, bring to the boil, then reduce heat and simmer for 40 minutes. Return chicken to skillet and simmer for 20 minutes longer or until chicken and chickpeas (garbanzo beans) are tender. Just prior to serving, sprinkle with almonds and parsley.

Serves 4

Redcurrant Duck,
Chickpea Ragout

SALADS

Served with crusty bread and a salad of mixed lettuces, chicken salads are the most delicious of summer meals. In this chapter you will find recipes not only for chicken salads but also for a marvelous Creamy Roast Duck Salad and an elegant Spinach and Chicken Liver Salad.

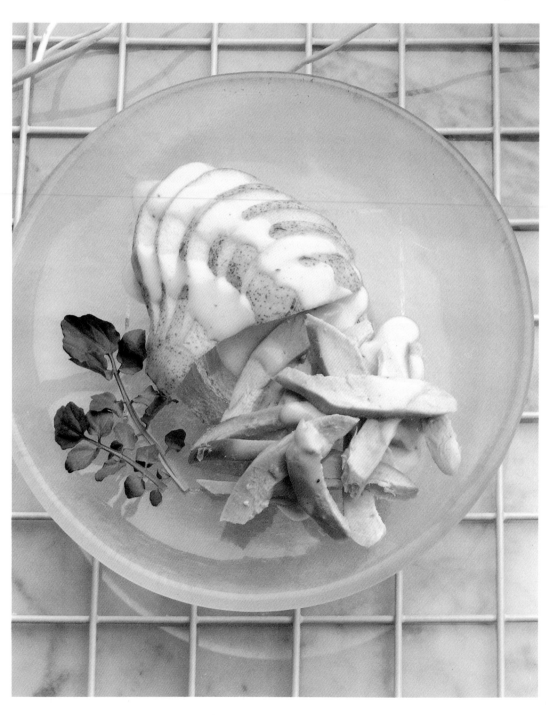

Fruity Smoked Chicken Salad

Fruity Smoked Chicken Salad

2 ripe pears, cored and halved vertically
1 x 3 pound/1.5 kg smoked chicken,
skin removed, cut into strips

WATERCRESS DRESSING
2 tablespoons/30 g butter
1 small bunch watercress
4 spring onions, chopped
1 clove garlic, crushed
2 teaspoons tarragon vinegar
1 tablespoon dry white wine
1 cup/250 mL heavy cream

1   To make dressing, melt butter in a
saucepan, stir in watercress, spring onions,
garlic, vinegar and white wine and bring
to simmering over a medium heat.
Simmer for 5 minutes, then stir in cream
and simmer, uncovered, for 10 minutes
longer or until dressing reduces and
thickens. Remove from heat and set aside
to cool for 10 minutes. Place dressing in a
food processor or blender and process
until smooth. Set aside to cool
completely.

2   Cut each pear half into slices vertically
from the bottom without cutting through
top. Fan pear and arrange attractively on
plate with chicken. Spoon dressing over
chicken and serve immediately.

Serves 4 as a starter or light meal

Smoked chicken is one of the
more recent food products
and is available from some
supermarkets and
delicatessens. It has been
cured and smoked and has
a pale pink flesh with a
delicate flavor.

Tomato and Chicken Salad

1 loaf unsliced wholegrain bread
3 tablespoons olive oil
4 slices bacon, cut into strips
1 cooked chicken, skin removed and
flesh cut into bite-sized pieces
8 oz/250 g cherry tomatoes,
cut into quarters
2 spring onions, finely chopped
freshly ground black pepper
6 fresh basil sprigs

BASIL MAYONNAISE
1 clove garlic, crushed
2 oz/60 g fresh basil leaves
1 cup/250 g mayonnaise

1   Remove crusts from bread and cut
into 1-inch/2.5 cm cubes. Place in a bowl
and sprinkle with olive oil. Toss to coat
bread cubes evenly with oil. Arrange
bread cubes in a single layer on a cookie
tray and bake for 10-15 minutes or until
golden and toasted. Set aside to cool.

2   Cook bacon in a skillet for 4-5 minutes
or until crisp. Remove bacon from skillet,
drain on paper towels and set aside to
cool.

3   To make mayonnaise, place garlic,
basil leaves and 1 tablespoon mayonnaise
in a food processor or blender and process
to purée. Add remaining mayonnaise and
process to combine.

4   Place chicken, tomatoes, spring
onions, black pepper to taste and half the
bacon in a large salad bowl. Top with
mayonnaise and toss to coat all
ingredients. Divide salad between six
plates, place croutons around edge of each
plate, sprinkle with remaining bacon and
garnish with basil sprigs.

Oven temperature
350°F, 180°C

This easy-to-prepare chicken
salad is a main course meal
in itself that needs no other
accompaniment.

Serves 6 as a main meal

WARM ORIENTAL CHICKEN SALAD

The best way to cook a chicken for a chicken salad is to place it breast side down in a saucepan. Pour over enough cold water just to cover the bird. Cut 1 onion into thick slices and add to pan with 4 peppercorns and several sprigs of parsley. Bring to the boil over a medium heat, then reduce heat, cover and simmer for 45 minutes or until chicken is cooked. Transfer chicken and cooking liquid to a large bowl. Ensure that chicken is breast side down in the bowl so that the breast flesh remains moist. Cover and refrigerate until cold.

7 oz/220 g cellophane or
transparent noodles
boiling water
1 cooked chicken, skin removed
and flesh shredded
1 carrot, shredded
3 tablespoons chopped cilantro
(fresh coriander)
1 cucumber, chopped
1 oz/30 g peanuts, chopped

PEANUT DRESSING
2 cloves garlic, crushed
$^1/_4$ cup/60 mL soy sauce
$^1/_4$ cup/60 mL fresh lemon juice
1 tablespoon peanut butter
$^1/_3$ cup/90 mL vegetable oil
1 tablespoon brown sugar

1   Place noodles in a large heatproof bowl, pour over boiling water to cover and set aside for 10 minutes. Drain.

2   Place chicken, carrot, cilantro (fresh coriander) and cucumber in a bowl and mix to combine.

3   To make dressing, place garlic, soy sauce, lemon juice, peanut butter, oil and sugar in a small saucepan and bring to the boil, stirring, over a medium heat. Cook, stirring, for 3 minutes. Pour dressing over chicken and toss to combine.

4   Divide noodles between four plates, top with chicken mixture and sprinkle with peanuts. Serve immediately.

Serves 4 as a main meal

CHICKEN AND ORANGE SALAD

1 cooked chicken, skin removed and
flesh cut into bite-sized pieces
2 stalks celery, sliced
7 oz/220 g canned water chestnuts,
drained and halved
1 orange, segmented
1 red onion, chopped

TARRAGON DRESSING
1 tablespoon chopped fresh parsley
$^1/_3$ cup/90 mL safflower oil
1 clove garlic, crushed
$^1/_4$ cup/60 mL tarragon vinegar

1   Place chicken, celery, water chestnuts,
orange segments and onion in a salad
bowl. Toss gently to combine.

2   To make dressing, place parsley, oil,
garlic and vinegar in a screwtop jar, and
shake well to combine. Pour over salad
and toss gently.

Serves 4

Chunks of tender chicken,
pieces of crunchy celery and
water chestnuts team with
fresh-tasting orange
segments to make the
perfect summer lunch.

Chicken and Orange Salad

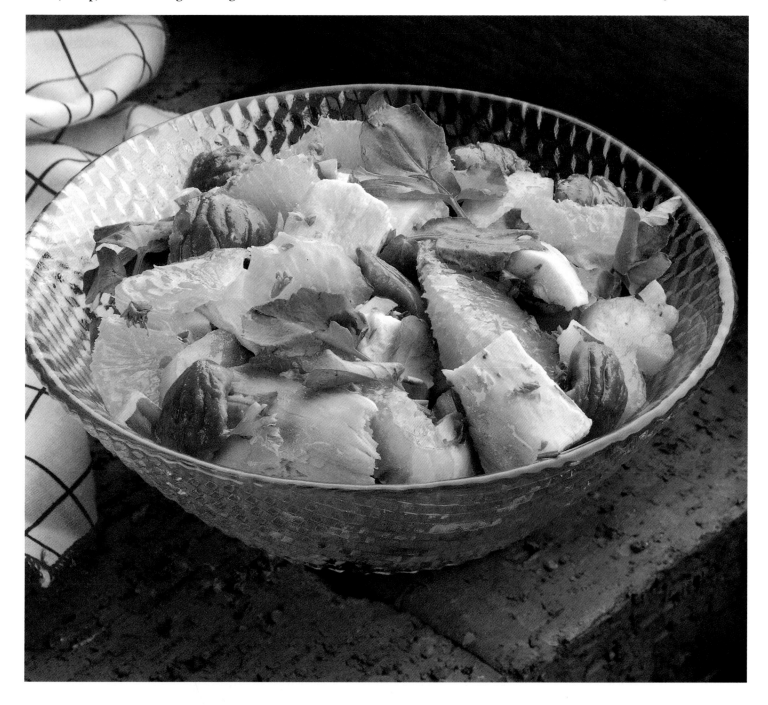

SPINACH AND CHICKEN LIVER SALAD

6 slices white bread, crusts removed
$^1/_4$ cup/$^1/_2$ stick/60 g butter
8 oz/250 g chicken livers, trimmed
3 tablespoons brandy
1 tablespoon dried mixed herbs
8 oz/250 g spinach, stalks
removed and discarded
$^1/_4$ cup/60 mL dry white wine
1 tablespoon olive oil
1 red pepper, finely chopped

1   Using cookie cutters, cut bread into decorative shapes. Melt half the butter in a skillet over a medium heat until bubbling. Add bread and cook for 1-2 minutes each side or until golden. Remove croutons from skillet and drain on paper towels.

2   Melt remaining butter in skillet and cook chicken livers, stirring constantly, for 2-3 minutes. Add brandy and herbs and cook for 3 minutes longer.

3   Arrange spinach on a large platter or in a salad bowl. Using a slotted spoon remove chicken livers from skillet, slice and scatter over spinach. Add wine to skillet and cook over a medium heat for 2 minutes, strain mixture into small bowl and discard any sediment. Add oil to strained mixture and mix to combine. Spoon dressing over salad, then top with croutons and red pepper.

Warm chicken livers, pretty-shaped croutons and spinach combine to make an attractive first course.

Spinach and Chicken Liver Salad

Serves 4 as a first course or light meal

CREAMY ROAST DUCK SALAD

1 x 4 pound/2 kg duck
freshly ground black pepper
2 tablespoons chopped fresh parsley

CREAMY ONION DRESSING
2 red onions, cut into wedges
2 tablespoons vegetable oil
³/4 cup/185 mL chicken stock
¹/2 cup/125 mL dry white wine
³/4 cup/185 g sour cream

1 Season duck with black pepper. Tuck wings under body of duck and tie legs together. Place bird breast side up on a wire rack set in a baking dish and bake for 1 hour or until duck is cooked. Remove from pan and set aside to cool completely.

2 To make dressing, separate onion wedges. Heat oil in a skillet and cook onions for 5 minutes or until soft. Stir in stock and cook for 8 minutes. Add wine, bring to the boil, then reduce heat and simmer, stirring to lift sediment from bottom of skillet, for 5 minutes. Remove skillet from heat, transfer contents to a bowl and set aside to cool to room temperature. Place sour cream in a bowl, add stock mixture and mix well to combine.

3 Remove skin from duck and discard. Strip flesh from duck, cut into bite-sized pieces and place in a bowl. Add dressing and toss to combine. Just prior to serving, sprinkle with parsley. Serve salad at room temperature or chilled.

Serves 4 as a light meal

Oven temperature
350°F, 180°C

Serve this delicious duck salad with boiled new potatoes or a plain rice dish and cold asparagus spears.

Creamy Roast Duck Salad

CHICKEN POTATO SALAD

Quick to prepare and sure to please, this substantial salad needs no other accompaniment. For the very hungry you might like to serve a salad of tossed assorted lettuces and fresh herbs, and thick slices of wholegrain bread. Fill pocket bread with leftover salad for a delicious lunch the next day.

Chicken Potato Salad

8 oz/250 g cooked chicken, skin removed, flesh cut into bite-sized pieces
4 zucchini, shredded
1 teaspoon chopped fresh thyme or $^1/_4$ teaspoon dried thyme
8 new potatoes, cooked and halved
1 red pepper, cut into strips
4 hard-boiled eggs, sliced
1 tablespoon chopped cilantro (fresh coriander) or parsley

CREAMY DRESSING
$^1/_4$ cup/60 mL French dressing
2 tablespoons mayonnaise
freshly ground black pepper

1   Place chicken, zucchini, thyme and potatoes in a bowl and toss to combine.

2   Divide chicken mixture between serving plates and top with red pepper and eggs.

3   To make dressing, place French dressing, mayonnaise and black pepper to taste in a small bowl and whisk to combine. Drizzle dressing over salad and sprinkle with cilantro or parsley.

Serves 4

CHICKEN AND THREE-RICE SALAD

4 cups/1 litre chicken stock
2 oz/60 g wild rice
2 oz/60 g brown rice
2 oz/60 g white rice
1 large spinach leaf, shredded
4 oz/125 g button mushrooms, sliced
4 spring onions, chopped
1 red pepper, cut into strips
2 tablespoons pine nuts, toasted
4 boneless chicken breasts, cooked
and sliced

CURRIED COCONUT DRESSING
$1/2$ cup/125 mL coconut milk
1 teaspoon grated fresh ginger
2 tablespoons white wine vinegar
2 teaspoons packed brown sugar
$1/2$ teaspoon curry powder
$1/4$ teaspoon turmeric
freshly ground black pepper

1   Place stock in a large saucepan and bring to the boil. Add wild and brown rice and cook for 25 minutes. Add white rice and cook for 15 minutes longer or until all grains are tender. Drain and rinse under cold running water.

2   Place rice, spinach, mushrooms, spring onions, red pepper, pine nuts and chicken in a bowl and toss to combine.

3   To make dressing, place coconut milk, ginger, vinegar, sugar, curry powder, turmeric and black pepper to taste in a screwtop jar and shake well to combine. Spoon dressing over salad and serve immediately.

Serves 4

Wild rice is the grain from an aquatic grass which grows in North America. It has a pleasant nutty flavor and takes 30-45 minutes to cook. The grains should burst when they are cooked.

Chicken and Three-Rice Salad

51

CRUNCHY CHICKEN SALAD

1 tablespoon vegetable oil
4 boneless chicken breasts
6 stalks celery, cut into strips
6 spring onions, chopped
$^1/_2$ cup/60 g roughly chopped pecans

SOUR CREAM DRESSING
1 cup/250 g dairy sour cream
$^1/_2$ cup/125 mL mayonnaise
freshly ground black pepper

1   To make dressing, place sour cream, mayonnaise and black pepper to taste in a bowl and whisk to combine.

2   Heat oil in a large skillet, add chicken and cook over a medium-high heat for 4-5 minutes each side or until cooked through. Remove chicken from skillet and set aside to cool. Cut cold chicken into strips.

3   Place chicken and dressing in a salad bowl and toss to coat. Add celery, spring onions and pecans to chicken mixture and toss well to combine. Cover and refrigerate for 1 hour before serving.

Serves 4

For a lower calorie (kilojoule) dressing replace the sour cream with plain yogurt and the mayonnaise with a low-oil mayonnaise.

Left: Crunchy Chicken Salad
Below: Chicken and Walnut Salad

CHICKEN AND WALNUT SALAD

¹/₂ cup/60 g chopped walnuts
1 x 3 pound/1.5 kg smoked chicken,
skin removed and flesh cut into strips
2 green apples

WALNUT VINAIGRETTE
¹/₄ cup/60 mL white wine vinegar
¹/₄ cup/60 mL walnut oil
1 tablespoon finely chopped cilantro
(fresh coriander)
freshly ground black pepper

1   Place walnuts in a shallow ovenproof dish and bake, stirring occasionally, for 15 minutes or until nuts are toasted. Remove from oven and set aside to cool.

2   To make vinaigrette, place vinegar, oil, cilantro (fresh coriander) and black pepper to taste in a screwtop jar and shake well to combine.

3   Cut apples into quarters, remove core then cut each quarter into three slices.

4   Place chicken, apples and walnuts in a salad bowl. Spoon vinaigrette over chicken mixture and toss well to combine. Serve immediately.

Serves 4

Oven temperature
350°F, 180°C

Walnuts can be roasted in the microwave. To roast in the microwave, place the walnuts on a glass or ceramic microwave-safe dish and cook, stirring every 2 minutes, on HIGH (100%) for 4-5 minutes or until nuts are roasted. Do not use a microwave-safe plastic container for roasting nuts as the oil that comes out of the nuts during roasting can cause the container to bubble or melt.

CHICKEN AND PINE NUT SALAD

1 tablespoon olive oil
4 boneless chicken breasts,
cut into strips
1 lettuce, leaves separated and torn
into pieces
1 carrot, cut into thin strips
2 tomatoes, cut into wedges
8 oz/250 g asparagus, blanched and cut
into 2-inch/5 cm lengths
2 tablespoons pine nuts, toasted
1 tablespoon snipped fresh chives

ORANGE DRESSING
$^1/_2$ cup/100 g plain yogurt
2 tablespoons orange juice
1 teaspoon finely grated orange rind
freshly ground black pepper

1   Heat oil in a large skillet, add chicken and stir-fry over a medium heat for 2-3 minutes or until cooked. Remove chicken from skillet, place on paper towels and set aside to cool.

2   To make dressing, place yogurt, orange juice, orange rind and black pepper to taste in a bowl and whisk to combine.

3   Arrange lettuce, carrot, tomatoes, asparagus and chicken attractively on a large serving platter. Sprinkle with pine nuts and chives, spoon over dressing and serve immediately.

Serves 4

Green beans or snow peas can be used in place of the asparagus in this salad if you wish.

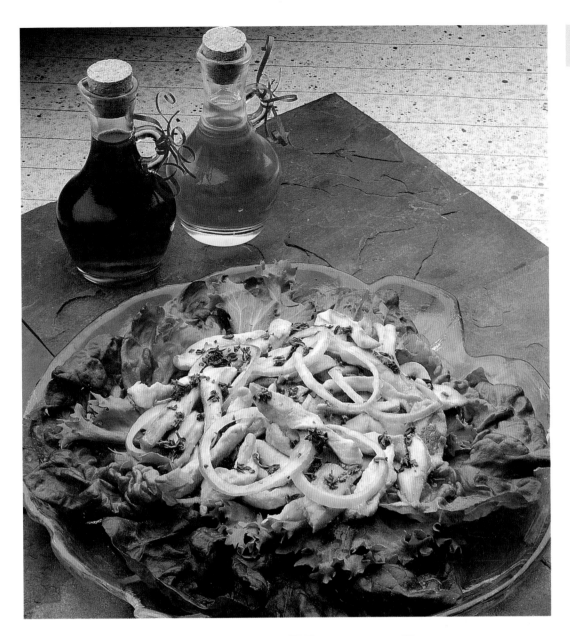

Far right: Chicken and Pine Nut Salad
Right: Chicken and Thyme Salad

CHICKEN AND THYME SALAD

2 tablespoons vegetable oil
6 boneless chicken breasts, cut into strips
2 tablespoons red wine vinegar
2 tablespoons olive oil
1 tablespoon chopped fresh thyme leaves
1 lettuce, leaves separated
$^1/_2$ bunch/250 g curly endive
2 red onions, sliced in rings

1   Heat vegetable oil in a large skillet, add chicken and stir-fry in batches for 5-6 minutes or until cooked. Remove chicken from skillet and set aside to cool.

2   Add vinegar to skillet and cook, stirring, for 1 minute. Strain liquid and place in a screwtop jar. Discard solids. Add olive oil and thyme to jar and shake well to combine.

3   Arrange lettuce and endive attractively on a large serving platter, top with chicken, then onion rings. Spoon dressing over salad and serve immediately.

Serves 8

Curly endive is a member of the chicory family. It has large, curly, frilly-edged leaves with a slightly bitter flavor. Use the paler heart leaves and stalks – the darker outside leaves can be very bitter and tough.

CURRIED CHICKEN SALAD

1 cup/250 mL dry white wine
1 cup/250 mL water
1 small onion, chopped
freshly ground black pepper
6 chicken pieces, skin removed
$^1/_2$ green pepper, diced
$^1/_2$ red pepper, diced
2 stalks celery, chopped
1 mango, sliced

CURRIED DRESSING
2 teaspoons vegetable oil
1 onion, sliced
1 teaspoon curry powder
$^3/_4$ cup/155 g plain yogurt
1 tablespoon chopped mango chutney

Serves 6

1 Place wine, water, onion and black pepper to taste in a saucepan and bring to simmering. Add chicken and poach for 30-35 minutes or until chicken is tender. Remove chicken from poaching liquid and chill. Strain liquid and refrigerate or freeze for using as stock in another recipe.

2 To make dressing, heat oil in a skillet, add onion and curry powder and cook, stirring, for 4-5 minutes or until onion is soft. Transfer to a small bowl, add yogurt and mango chutney and mix to combine.

3 Place cold chicken, red and green pepper and celery in a bowl. Spoon over dressing and toss gently to coat chicken pieces. Cover and chill until ready to serve. Just prior to serving, top salad with mango slices.

If fresh mangoes are unavailable this salad can be made using drained canned mangoes or a segmented orange instead.

CHICKEN AND VEGETABLE SALAD

1 pound/500 g broccoli, broken
into florets
2 carrots, sliced diagonally
1 cooked chicken, skin removed and
flesh cut into bite-sized pieces
1 avocado, stoned, peeled and chopped

GINGER DRESSING
1 tablespoon soy sauce
1 teaspoon grated fresh ginger
$^1/_2$ teaspoon sesame oil
$^1/_4$ cup/60 mL French dressing
freshly ground black pepper

Serves 6

1 Boil or microwave broccoli and carrots until just tender. Drain, refresh under cold running water, drain again and set aside to cool completely.

2 Place broccoli, carrots, chicken and avocado in a salad bowl.

3 To make dressing, place soy sauce, ginger, oil, French dressing and black pepper to taste in a screwtop jar and shake well to combine. Spoon dressing over salad and toss to combine.

Sesame oil is a strong-flavored oil extracted from sesame seeds that adds a nutty flavor to food. It is of Asian origin and is available from Asian food stores and some supermarkets. Care should be taken when using sesame oil, as a little adds a lot of taste.

Chicken and Melon Salad

Chicken and Melon Salad

1/4 small watermelon
1/2 honeydew melon
1/2 cantaloupe
1 x 3 pound/1.5 kg smoked chicken,
skin removed and flesh cut into strips
4 tablespoons chopped cilantro
(fresh coriander)
freshly ground black pepper
1/4 cup/60 mL French dressing

1   Remove skin and seeds from watermelon, honeydew melon and cantaloupe and cut flesh into batons.

2   Place watermelon, honeydew melon, cantaloupe and chicken in a bowl and toss to combine.

3   Sprinkle salad with cilantro (fresh coriander), season to taste with black pepper and spoon over French dressing. Toss to combine.

Serves 4

This salad is delicious made with any combination of melons – so choose your favorite ones or those that are available.

SNACKS

*Tacos, burgers and open sandwiches are
all wonderful snack foods or light meals. Homemade, using
chicken, they make healthy and nutritious alternatives
to commercial fast foods.*

Chicken Tacos

CHICKEN TACOS

1 tablespoon vegetable oil
1 large onion, finely chopped
2 cloves garlic, crushed
1 pound/500 g ground chicken
2 tablespoons (1 oz/30 g packet)
taco seasoning mix
$^{1}/_{2}$ cup/125 mL water
3 tablespoons taco sauce
8 taco shells, warmed
2 oz/60 g shredded Cheddar cheese

1   Heat oil in a large skillet and cook onion and garlic over a medium heat for 3-4 minutes or until onion is soft. Add chicken and cook, stirring, for 5-6 minutes or until chicken changes color. Stir in taco seasoning mix, water and taco sauce, bring to simmering and simmer for 4-5 minutes.

2   Divide chicken mixture between taco shells, top with shredded cheese and serve with extra taco sauce if desired.

Serves 4

Taco shells are a great store-cupboard item. This recipe could also be made using leftover roast chicken. If using cooked chicken, remove skin, and grind or finely chop chicken. Cook as in recipe but only cook chicken for 2-3 minutes.

BACON AND CHICKEN LIVER KEBABS

1 pound/500 g chicken livers, trimmed
$^{3}/_{4}$ cup/185 mL brandy
2 cloves garlic, crushed
7 oz/220 g slices bacon, rinds removed

1   Place chicken livers, brandy and garlic in a bowl and toss to combine. Cover and set aside to marinate for 1 hour. Drain chicken livers. Cut bacon slices in half and wrap around each liver.

2   Thread three bacon-wrapped livers onto lightly oiled bamboo skewers and cook under a preheated broiler for 2 minutes each side or until bacon is crisp and livers are cooked.

Serves 4

When cooking chicken livers, take care not to overcook them or they will be dry and tough. Perfectly cooked chicken liver should still be slightly pink inside.

Healthy Chicken Burgers

HEALTHY CHICKEN BURGERS

A burger made with lots of healthy salad ingredients and a patty of lean chicken is just the right snack or light meal for weekend fare. If you cannot purchase ground chicken, you can make your own using 1 pound/500 g boneless chicken breasts. Remove skin from breasts before grinding.

4 thick slices tomato
4 hamburger buns, split and toasted
8 slices cucumber
4 lettuce leaves
1 oz/30 g alfalfa sprouts

CHICKEN PATTIES
1 pound/500 g ground chicken
1 egg, lightly beaten
$^1/_2$ cup/30 g bread crumbs,
made from stale bread
2 teaspoons Worcestershire sauce
2 tablespoons/30 g butter

1 To make patties, place ground chicken, egg, bread crumbs and Worcestershire sauce in a bowl and mix to combine. Shape mixture into eight patties, place on a plate, cover and refrigerate for 20-30 minutes.

2 Melt butter in a large skillet and cook patties, pressing down with a spatula, for 3-4 minutes each side or until cooked. Remove patties from skillet and drain on paper towels.

3 To assemble burgers, place a tomato slice on the bottom half of each bun, top with 2 patties, 2 cucumber slices, a lettuce leaf, a few alfalfa sprouts and top half of bun. Serve immediately.

Serves 4

CHICKEN AND PEPPER TORTILLAS

3 tablespoons tomato paste (purée)
4 oz/125 g shredded Cheddar cheese
8 oz/250 g chopped cooked chicken
$^1/_2$ green pepper, chopped
1 fresh red chili, seeds removed
and chopped

TORTILLAS
$1^1/_2$ cups/250 g corn meal
$1^1/_2$ cups/185 g all-purpose flour
pinch salt
5 tablespoons butter, chopped
$^3/_4$ cup/185 mL warm water

1 To make Tortillas, place corn meal, flour, salt and butter in a food processor and process until mixture resembles fine bread crumbs. With machine running, slowly add water to form a dough. Turn dough onto a lightly floured surface and knead for 2 minutes.

2 Roll out dough and, using a 4-inch/10 cm round cutter, cut out eight circles. Place rounds on a lightly greased cookie sheet and bake for 10 minutes.

3 Spread each tortilla with tomato paste (purée), sprinkle with cheese, chicken, green pepper and chili and bake for 10 minutes.

Makes 8 tortillas

Oven temperature
350°F, 180°C

In Mexico, thin pancakes made of corn meal are called tortillas, while in Spain a tortilla is a flat omelette.

Chicken and Pepper Tortillas

BUTTERMILK MUFFINS WITH TURKEY

Oven temperature
350°F, 180°C

Buttermilk is a cultured dairy product that has the same food value as skim milk. It is a useful low-fat ingredient that is sometimes used in baked goods.

$^1/_4$ cup/$^1/_2$ stick/60 g butter
8 oz/250 g sliced smoked turkey
$^1/_2$ cup/155 g guava, apple
or redcurrant jelly

BUTTERMILK MUFFINS
$^1/_2$ cup/1 stick/125 g butter
$^1/_2$ cup/100 g superfine sugar
2 eggs
2 oz/60 g golden raisins, chopped
2 oz/60 g walnuts, chopped
1 teaspoon baking soda
1 cup/250 mL buttermilk or milk
2 cups/250 g all-purpose flour, sifted

1   To make muffins, place butter and sugar in a bowl and beat until creamy. Add eggs, one at a time, beating well after each addition. Stir in golden raisins and walnuts. Dissolve baking soda in buttermilk or milk. Fold flour and milk mixture, alternately, into creamed mixture.

2   Spoon batter into greased muffin pans and cook for 12 minutes or until golden and cooked when tested with a skewer. Turn on a wire rack to cool.

3   Split muffins, spread lightly with butter. Top bottom half with turkey slices, guava jelly and top of muffin.

Makes 15 muffins

Buttermilk Muffins with Turkey

62

Grilled Avocado Sandwiches

GRILLED AVOCADO SANDWICHES

4 thick slices whole wheat bread
2 oz/60 g cream cheese, softened
4 tablespoons mayonnaise
8 oz/250 g cooked chicken, sliced
4 slices Cheddar cheese
1 avocado, stoned, peeled and sliced
1 tablespoon snipped fresh chives

1   Spread each slice of bread with cream cheese, then mayonnaise. Top with chicken and a cheese slice. Cook under a preheated grill for 2-3 minutes or until cheese melts.

2   Top with avocado slices, sprinkle with chives and serve immediately.

Serves 4

TURKEY TRIANGLES

Oven temperature
425°F, 220°C

It is worth making double the quantity of this recipe so that you can freeze the triangles to have on hand for snacks and light meals. Freeze triangles in an airtight freezerproof container or sealed freezer bag. Reheat in oven at 350°F/180°C for 10-15 minutes or until heated.

5 oz/155 g prepared puff pastry

TURKEY FILLING
4 slices smoked turkey, chopped
2 tablespoons dairy sour cream
1 tablespoon cranberry sauce
2 teaspoons snipped fresh chives
freshly ground black pepper

1   Roll out pastry to $^1/_8$-inch/3 mm thickness and cut into four 5-inch/12 cm squares.

2   To make filling, place turkey, sour cream, cranberry sauce, chives and black pepper to taste in a small bowl and mix to combine. Place a spoonful of filling in the centre of each pastry square. Fold opposite pastry corners together to form a triangle. Brush edges with a little water and press together, using a fork to seal and make a decorative edge. Place on a greased baking tray and bake for 15 minutes or until pastry is puffed and golden.

Makes 4 triangles

Left: Turkey Triangles
Below: Turkey and Stilton Sandwiches

TURKEY AND STILTON SANDWICHES

1 French bread stick, cut into
12 thick slices
2 tablespoons Dijon mustard
12 slices smoked turkey
6^1/$_2$ oz/200 g Stilton cheese, crumbled
1 oz/30 g watercress, broken into sprigs

Spread each slice of bread with mustard. Top with turkey and cheese and garnish with watercress. Serve immediately.

Serves 6

Every country seems to have its own favorite blue cheese. Stilton is the blue cheese of Britain. For these sandwiches you can choose your favorite blue cheese. If you do not like blue cheese you might like to use Brie, Camembert or a cream cheese instead.

CHICKEN DONER KEBABS

2 tablespoons/30 g butter
4 boneless chicken thighs, cut into
thin strips
2 teaspoons curry powder
$^1/_2$ teaspoon sweet chili sauce
2 tablespoons ketchup
4 large pita bread rounds, warmed
1 bunch/250 g watercress, broken
into sprigs
1 red onion, sliced
1 tomato, sliced

These homemade kebabs
are sure to be a winner with
friends and family. They are
also delicious cold. If making
to serve cold allow the
chicken mixture to cool
before assembling kebabs.

1   Melt butter in a skillet, add chicken
and stir-fry for 3 minutes or until color
changes. Stir in curry powder, chili sauce
and ketchup and cook for 1 minute
longer.

2   Divide chicken mixture between pita
bread rounds, top with watercress, onion
and tomato, then roll up to enclose the
filling.

Serves 4

Chicken Doner Kebabs

Cheesy Chicken Pastries

CHEESY CHICKEN PASTRIES

12 oz/375 g prepared shortcrust pastry
2 tablespoons milk

CHICKEN FILLING
2 tablespoons/30 g butter
1 clove garlic, crushed
2 boneless chicken breasts, chopped
8 button mushrooms, sliced
6 stalks asparagus, chopped
2 tablespoons dairy sour cream
2 oz/60 g shredded Cheddar cheese
2 tablespoons grated Parmesan cheese
1 tablespoon chopped fresh parsley
freshly ground black pepper

1 Roll out pastry to $^1/_8$-in/3 mm thickness and, using an upturned saucer as a guide, cut out ten $5^1/_4$-in/13 cm circles. Set aside.

2 To make filling, melt 1 tablespoon butter in a skillet over a medium-high heat, add garlic and chicken and stir-fry for 3-4 minutes or until chicken is just cooked. Remove chicken from skillet and set aside to cool. Melt remaining butter in skillet, add mushrooms and asparagus and cook over a high heat for 3-4 minutes or until asparagus is tender crisp. Remove vegetable mixture from skillet and set aside to cool.

3 Place chicken mixture, vegetable mixture, sour cream, Cheddar cheese and Parmesan cheese, parsley and black pepper to taste in a bowl and mix to combine. Place a spoonful of chicken mixture in the centre of each pastry round and brush edge of pastry with a little water. Draw edges together over top of filling, press to seal and crimp edges with fingertips to form a fluted pattern.

4 Brush pastry parcels with a little milk, place on a greased cookie sheet and bake for 20-25 minutes or until golden brown.

Makes 10 pastries

Oven temperature
400°F, 200°C

Keep a store of these delicious pastries in your freezer – you will always have a tasty snack to hand. Serve unaccompanied for a snack, or with a salad for a light meal.

QUICK MEALS

Chicken is ideal for those times when a substantial meal is required but time is short. This chapter provides recipes to fit that bill perfectly. It is filled with wonderful ideas for quick family meals and impromptu entertaining.

Chicken Waldorf Loaf

CHICKEN WALDORF LOAF

1 round loaf bread
1 Granny Smith apple, finely chopped
2 oz/60 g walnuts, chopped
3 spring onions, finely chopped
2 tablespoons chopped fresh parsley
$^1/_2$ cup/125 g mayonnaise
freshly ground black pepper
10 spinach leaves, stalks removed
and discarded
3 boneless chicken breasts,
cooked and sliced
4 tomatoes, sliced

1   Cut top off the loaf and scoop out middle, so that only the crust remains as a large bread case. Reserve top of loaf. The crumbs from the centre will not be used in this recipe, but can be made into bread crumbs.

2   Place apple, walnuts, spring onions, parsley, mayonnaise and black pepper to taste in a bowl and mix to combine. Place a layer of spinach leaves in bottom of bread case, top with a layer of chicken, a layer of apple mixture and finally a layer of tomato slices. Repeat layers, ending with a layer of spinach, until all ingredients are used and loaf is filled. Replace top and wrap loaf in aluminum foil. Place a board on top of loaf, weight down and refrigerate overnight. Serve cut into wedges.

Serves 8

A perfect picnic dish –
delicate chicken breasts are
combined with Waldorf
salad ingredients, placed in
a bread case, wrapped in
aluminum foil and
refrigerated overnight. All
you have to do in the
morning is pack the picnic
basket and you are ready
to go.

CRUSTY PARMESAN DRUMSTICKS

3 tablespoons Dijon mustard
4 tablespoons vegetable oil
4 spring onions, finely chopped
1 oz/30 g grated fresh Parmesan cheese
freshly ground black pepper
8 chicken drumsticks
$^1/_2$ cup/30 g bread crumbs, made from
stale bread
$^1/_4$ cup/$^1/_2$ stick/60 g butter, melted

1   Place mustard, oil, spring onions, Parmesan cheese and black pepper to taste in a bowl and mix to combine.

2   Brush each drumstick with mustard mixture, then roll in bread crumbs and place in a lightly greased baking dish. Pour butter over drumsticks and bake for 30 minutes or until drumsticks are cooked.

Serves 4

Oven temperature
350°F, 180°C

Crispy on the outside and
moist inside, these drumsticks
are a popular family meal.
Serve with mashed potatoes
and a green salad for one of
the easiest meals you will
ever make.

TURKEY CROQUETTES

^{1}/3 cup/90 g butter
1^1/3 cups/170 g all-purpose flour
1 cup/250 mL hot milk
4 oz/125 g ricotta cheese
8 oz/250 g cooked turkey, chopped
^{1}/2 cup/60 g shredded Cheddar cheese
2 tablespoons chopped fresh parsley
1 cup/125 g dried bread crumbs
1 egg, lightly beaten
oil for deep-frying

Croquettes are a great way to use any leftover poultry or meat. In this recipe turkey has been used, but you could use leftover chicken, lamb or beef. Canned tuna or salmon are delicious alternatives. If using canned food, drain off any liquid first.

Turkey Croquettes

1   Melt butter in a saucepan, stir in ^{1}/3 cup/45 g flour and cook, stirring, for 30 seconds. Whisk in milk and cook, stirring, over a medium heat for 4-5 minutes or until mixture thickens. Remove pan from heat and stir in ricotta cheese, turkey, Cheddar cheese and parsley. Mix well to combine and refrigerate until completely cold.

2   Place bread crumbs and remaining flour on separate plates and set aside. Shape turkey mixture into croquette shapes, roll each croquette in flour, then dip in egg and roll in bread crumbs. Place on a plate lined with plastic food wrap, cover and chill for 15 minutes.

3   Heat oil in a large saucepan until hot and cook croquettes for 3-4 minutes or until golden.

Serves 4

CHICKEN SAUTE

2 tablespoons vegetable oil
1 onion, sliced
1 green pepper, cut into strips
1 red pepper, cut into strips
1 zucchini, sliced
1½ cups/375 mL tomato purée
1 tablespoon chopped fresh basil
1 tablespoon chopped fresh parsley
1 teaspoon chopped fresh thyme or
½ teaspoon dried thyme
1 pound/500 g boneless chicken breasts,
cut into strips
freshly ground black pepper

1   Heat oil in a large skillet and cook onion over a medium heat for 5 minutes or until soft. Add green and red pepper, zucchini and tomato purée and bring to the boil, then reduce heat and simmer for 10 minutes.

2   Stir in basil, parsley, thyme and chicken and cook for 10 minutes or until chicken is cooked. Season to taste with black pepper.

Serves 4

A medley of summer vegetables and chicken makes a quick and easy sauté that is delicious served with boiled noodles tossed in butter and finely chopped fresh parsley.

Chicken with Curry Sauce

CHICKEN WITH CURRY SAUCE

Spatchcocking a bird means to split and flatten it. The easiest way to cut the bird is to use a pair of poultry shears. First cut off the wing tips then cut the bird along each side of the backbone to remove it. Now place the bird breast side up and using the heel of your hand push down sharply to flatten the bird and break the breastbone. To ensure that the bird holds its shape during cooking, thread two skewers through it. One skewer is threaded through the legs, avoiding the bones, and the other through the wings and breast.

$^1/_4$ cup/$^1/_2$ stick/60 g butter
4 boneless chicken breasts,
skin removed
1 onion, chopped
1 clove garlic, crushed
1 tablespoon curry powder
$^1/_2$ teaspoon ground cumin
$^1/_2$ teaspoon ground coriander
1 tablespoon honey
1 tablespoon fresh lemon juice
$^1/_3$ cup/90 mL red wine
$^3/_4$ cup/185 mL heavy cream
2 tablespoons mayonnaise
2 tablespoons chopped cilantro
(fresh coriander)

Serves 4

1   Melt butter in a large skillet and cook chicken over a medium heat for 3-4 minutes each side or until cooked. Remove chicken from skillet, set aside and keep warm.

2   Add onion and garlic to skillet and cook for 3-4 minutes or until onion is soft. Stir in curry powder, cumin and ground coriander, and cook for 2 minutes longer.

3   Stir in honey, lemon juice and wine, and cook for 2 minutes, then stir in cream and mayonnaise, and simmer for 2 minutes longer. Spoon sauce over chicken, sprinkle with cilantro (fresh coriander) and serve immediately.

HONEY CHICKEN

1 x 3 pound/1.5 kg chicken

HONEY GLAZE
3 tablespoons honey
2 teaspoons ground ginger
3 tablespoons Worcestershire sauce
2 tablespoons soy sauce
2 cloves garlic, crushed

1 Preheat broiler to medium. Spatchcock chicken (see hint opposite) and place on a cookie sheet.

2 To make glaze, place honey, ginger, Worcestershire sauce, soy sauce and garlic in a small saucepan and bring to the boil over a medium heat. Brush glaze over chicken and cook under broiler for 10-15 minutes each side or until chicken is cooked.

Serves 4

Honey Chicken

REDCURRANT HENS

Oven temperature
350°F, 180°C

2 Rock Cornish hens, cut in
half, lengthwise

REDCURRANT GLAZE
1 tablespoon/15 g butter
4 tablespoons redcurrant jelly
2 teaspoons honey
3 tablespoons fresh lemon juice

1   To make glaze, place butter,
redcurrant jelly, honey and lemon juice in
a small saucepan and cook, stirring, over a
medium heat until all ingredients are
melted and combined.

2   Place birds in a baking dish, brush
with glaze and bake, occasionally
brushing with glaze, for 25 minutes or
until birds are cooked.

Serves 4

CHINESE CHICKEN WINGS

You might like to make baby
drumsticks from the chicken
wings. This makes them very
easy to eat – especially for
children or if serving as finger
food.
To make baby drumsticks,
first cut off the wings tips,
then, holding the small end
of the bone and using a
sharp knife, cut around the
bone to free the meat. Next
cut, scrape and push meat
down to large end of bone.
Using your fingers pull the skin
and meat down over end of
bone so that the wing
resembles a little drumstick.

$^{1}/_{4}$ cup/$^{1}/_{2}$ stick/60 g butter
1 clove garlic, crushed
1 tablespoon grated fresh ginger
16 chicken wings
3 tablespoons honey
3 tablespoons Worcestershire sauce
3 tablespoons soy sauce
3 tablespoons sesame seeds

1   Melt butter in a large skillet and cook
garlic and ginger over a medium heat for
1 minute.

2   Add chicken wings and cook, stirring,
for 3 minutes. Stir in honey,
Worcestershire sauce and soy sauce and
cook for 5 minutes longer or until
chicken wings are cooked. Stir in sesame
seeds and serve immediately.

Serves 4

Chinese Chicken Wings,
Redcurrant Hens

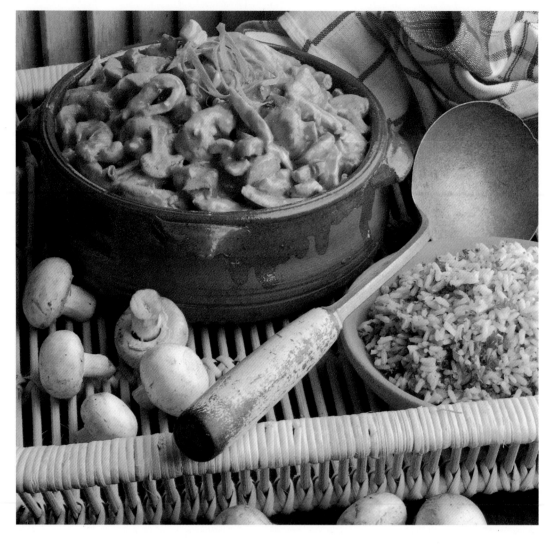

Chicken Stroganoff

CHICKEN STROGANOFF

$^1/_3$ cup/90 g butter
1 pound/500 g boneless chicken breasts,
cut into strips
5 oz/155 g button mushrooms, halved
$^1/_2$ cup/125 mL dry white wine
1 cup/250 mL heavy cream
2 tablespoons tomato paste (purée)
$^1/_2$ teaspoon ground nutmeg
1 spring onion, finely chopped

1   Melt $^1/_4$ cup/$^1/_2$ stick/60 g butter in a skillet and cook chicken, stirring, over a medium heat for 2-3 minutes or until chicken just changes color. Remove chicken from skillet and set aside.

2   Melt remaining butter in skillet and cook mushrooms for 2-3 minutes, then stir in wine, cream, tomato paste (purée) and nutmeg. Cook, stirring, over a high heat for 5 minutes or until sauce reduces and thickens slightly.

3   Add chicken to mushroom mixture and cook, stirring, over a medium heat, for 3-4 minutes or until chicken is cooked. Stir in spring onion and serve immediately.

Serves 4

Serve Chicken Stroganoff on a bed of boiled white or brown rice accompanied by a seasonal green vegetable – asparagus or green beans are delicious.

CHICKEN CASSEROLE

2 tablespoons vegetable oil
4 boneless chicken breasts,
cut into strips
1 turnip, cut into strips
2 onions, chopped
14 oz/440 g canned red peppers, drained
and cut into strips
1 cup/250 mL dry white wine
14 oz/440 g canned tomatoes,
undrained and mashed
3 tablespoons chopped fresh basil

1   Heat oil in a large skillet and cook chicken over a medium heat, stirring, for 2-3 minutes or until chicken just changes color. Remove chicken from skillet and set aside.

2   Add turnip, onions and red peppers to skillet and cook for 3-4 minutes. Stir in wine and tomatoes and bring to the boil over a medium heat, stirring, then reduce heat and simmer, uncovered, for 10 minutes or until turnip is tender. Return chicken to skillet and cook for 3-4 minutes longer or until chicken is cooked. Stir in basil and serve immediately.

All this easy chicken dish needs to make a complete meal is hot garlic bread or crusty bread rolls and a salad of mixed lettuce and herbs.

Chicken Casserole   **Serves 4**

VEGETABLE PAN-FRY

2 tablespoons vegetable oil
1 onion, chopped
1 green pepper, chopped
4 oz/125 g mushrooms, sliced
8 oz/250 g chicken livers, chopped
2 large tomatoes, peeled and chopped
2 fresh sage leaves, chopped
freshly ground black pepper
8 oz/250 g bow pasta, cooked

1   Heat oil in a large skillet and cook onion for 3-4 minutes or until soft. Add green pepper and cook, stirring, for 3-4 minutes, then add mushrooms and cook for 2 minutes longer.

2   Add chicken livers and cook, stirring, for 3-4 minutes or until livers change color. Stir in tomatoes, sage and black pepper to taste and cook, stirring constantly, for 4-5 minutes or until juice starts to run from tomatoes.

3   Add pasta to skillet and cook for 4-5 minutes longer or until pasta is heated. Serve immediately.

Serves 4

A great way to use leftover pasta, this dish could be made using any small pasta shapes.

Vegetable Pan-Fry

78

CHICKEN PANCAKES

1 cup/125 g all-purpose flour
1 egg
1^1/$_2$ cups/375 mL milk
1 zucchini, shredded
2 tablespoons chopped fresh parsley

CHICKEN TOPPING
1 cup/250 mL heavy cream
^{1}/$_4$ teaspoon ground nutmeg
^{1}/$_4$ cup/60 mL white wine
8 oz/250 g cooked chicken, cut
into pieces
1 tablespoon snipped fresh chives

Chicken Pancakes   **Serves 4**

1   Place flour, egg and milk in a food processor or blender and process until smooth. Transfer mixture to a bowl and stir in zucchini and parsley. Cover and set aside to stand for 15 minutes.

2   Pour enough mixture into a heated, greased small skillet to just cover the bottom and cook over a medium-high heat, until bubbles form on the surface. Turn pancake and cook until golden brown. Repeat with remaining mixture.

3   To make topping, place cream in a saucepan and cook over a medium heat for 4-5 minutes or until cream is hot. Stir in nutmeg and wine and bring to simmering, then simmer for 10 minutes or until mixture reduces and thickens slightly. Stir in chicken and chives and cook for 2-3 minutes longer. To serve, spoon topping over pancakes.

For brunch, lunch or supper, pancakes are a great light meal. Grated zucchini and chopped parsley in the batter make these pancakes deliciously different.

Oven temperature
350°F, 180°C

BAKED CHICKEN AIOLI

3 pounds/1.5 kg chicken pieces
$^1/_2$ cup/125 mL olive oil
$^1/_4$ cup/60 mL lemon juice
1 onion, finely chopped
2 tablespoons chopped fresh parsley

AIOLI
4 cloves garlic, crushed
2 egg yolks
2 tablespoons lemon juice
freshly ground black pepper
1 cup/250 mL olive oil

1   To make Aioli, place garlic, egg yolks, lemon juice and black pepper to taste in a food processor or blender and process to combine. With machine running, slowly pour in oil until mayonnaise is thick and creamy. Transfer Aioli to a bowl, cover and refrigerate until required.

2   Place chicken pieces in a shallow ovenproof dish. Place olive oil and lemon juice in a small bowl and whisk to combine. Pour oil mixture over chicken, cover and set aside to marinate for 1 hour.

3   Remove cover and bake chicken for 1 hour or until golden and cooked through. To serve, sprinkle chicken with chopped onion and parsley and accompany with Aioli.

Serves 6

This garlicky mayonnaise is also delicious served as a dip for raw and lightly cooked vegetables or as a salad accompaniment.

CHICKEN TERIYAKI

1 tablespoon vegetable oil
3 tablespoons soy sauce
3 tablespoons Worcestershire sauce
2 tablespoons red wine vinegar
$^{3}/_{4}$ cup/185 mL dry sherry
2 tablespoons packed brown sugar
2 cloves garlic, crushed
4 boneless chicken breasts, cut into strips
4 red peppers, cut into thin strips

YOGURT CHILI SAUCE
$^{1}/_{2}$ cup/100 g plain yogurt
1 tablespoon lime juice
$^{1}/_{4}$ teaspoon sambal oelek (chili paste)

1   Heat oil in a large skillet, add soy sauce, Worcestershire sauce, vinegar, sherry, sugar and garlic and cook, stirring, for 2 minutes.

2   Add chicken and red peppers to skillet and cook, stirring, for 5-8 minutes or until chicken is cooked and sauce thickens slightly.

3   To make sauce, place yogurt, lime juice and sambal oelek (chili paste) in a bowl and mix to combine.

Serves 4

For a complete meal serve with boiled brown rice and a green vegetable such as beans, broccoli or cabbage.

BASIL CHICKEN

1 tablespoon olive oil
4 boneless chicken breasts, cut
into strips
2 leeks, white part only, sliced
4 oz/125 g button mushrooms, sliced
6 sun-dried tomatoes, drained and sliced
2 tablespoons red wine vinegar
3 tablespoons lime or lemon juice
1 small red chili, seeded and chopped
1 tablespoon chopped fresh basil
1 tablespoon chopped fresh parsley

This dish is delicious served
with boiled noodles or pasta
of your choice and a tossed
green salad.

1   Heat oil in a large skillet over a
medium heat, add chicken and stir-fry for
5 minutes or until chicken is just cooked.
Remove chicken from skillet, set aside
and keep warm.

2   Add leeks, mushrooms, sun-dried
tomatoes, vinegar, lime or lemon juice,
chili, basil and parsley to skillet and cook,
stirring, for 3 minutes.

3   Return chicken to skillet and cook,
stirring, for 2-3 minutes longer.

Serves 4

Left: Basil Chicken
Below: Honey Chicken Kebabs

HONEY CHICKEN KEBABS

1 tablespoon/15 g butter
1 tablespoon honey
3 tablespoons lemon juice
2 teaspoons apricot jam
2 teaspoons finely grated lemon rind
freshly ground black pepper
4 boneless chicken breasts, cut
into ³/4-inch/2 cm cubes
2 red peppers, cut into
³/4-inch/2 cm cubes

YOGURT SAUCE
¹/2 cup/100 g plain yogurt
1 tablespoon lemon juice
1 clove garlic, crushed
¹/4 teaspoon ground coriander
¹/4 teaspoon ground cumin

1   Melt butter in a large skillet over a medium heat, add honey, lemon juice, apricot jam, lemon rind and black pepper to taste and cook, stirring, for 1-2 minutes or until honey and jam are melted and mixture is combined.

2   Thread chicken and red pepper cubes, alternately, onto eight lightly oiled bamboo skewers. Place skewers in skillet and cook, turning frequently, for 7-10 minutes or until chicken is cooked through.

3   To make sauce, place yogurt, lemon juice, garlic, coriander, cumin and black pepper to taste in bowl and mix to combine.

4   To serve, place kebabs on a bed of rice, spoon over sauce and serve immediately.

Serves 4

For something different you might like to serve these kebabs on a bed of yellow rice. To achieve the yellow color add a little ground turmeric to the water before cooking.

PEPPERED CHICKEN

2 tablespoons cracked black peppercorns
8 boneless chicken breasts
$^1/_4$ cup/$^1/_2$ stick/60 g butter
$^1/_2$ cup/125 mL dry sherry
1 cup/250 mL heavy cream

1   Sprinkle peppercorns over chicken breasts and lightly pound to slightly flatten the chicken.

2   Melt butter in a large skillet over a medium heat, add chicken to skillet and cook for 4-5 minutes each side or until chicken is cooked through. Remove chicken from skillet, set aside and keep warm.

3   Add sherry and cream to skillet, bring to the boil, reduce heat and simmer for 10-15 minutes or until sauce is reduced by half. Spoon sauce over chicken and serve.

Serves 4

A quick and delicious dish that is ideal for impromptu entertaining. For a complete meal serve with crusty bread or rolls, steamed green beans and cherry tomatoes.

Indonesian Chicken

3 tablespoons vegetable oil
4 boneless chicken breasts, cut into
$^3/_4$-inch/2 cm cubes
8 oz/250 g green beans, cut into
1-inch/2.5 cm pieces
$^1/_4$ cup/60 mL lemon juice
2 tablespoons soy sauce
1 tablespoon packed brown sugar
2 teaspoons ground turmeric
$^1/_2$ cup/125 mL water

1 Heat oil in a wok or skillet, add chicken and stir-fry for 3-4 minutes or until chicken browns. Remove chicken from skillet and set aside.

2 Add beans to pan and stir-fry for 2 minutes. Stir in lemon juice, soy sauce, sugar, turmeric and water, bring to the boil and simmer for 3-5 minutes or until beans are tender and sauce reduces and thickens slightly. Return chicken to pan and cook for 2-3 minutes longer or until chicken is cooked through.

Serves 4

For successful stir-frying, heat your wok until very hot, then add the oil, swirl the wok to coat the surface, continue to heat until the oil is almost smoking before adding the food. Following this procedure will ensure that the food does not stick to the wok. The exception to this is when the first ingredients to be added to the wok are garlic, spring onions, ginger or chilies. Add these ingredients immediately after adding the oil or they will burn.

CHICKEN WITH PEANUTS

1 pound/500 g chicken breasts, cut
into 1-inch/2.5 cm cubes
$^1/_3$ cup/90 mL dry white wine
1 teaspoon grated fresh ginger
1 clove garlic, crushed
1 tablespoon vegetable oil
1 cup/250 mL chicken stock
$^1/_3$ cup/90 g crunchy peanut butter
2 spring onions, cut into thin strips
1 red chili, sliced

For a complete meal, serve
this easy chicken dish with
boiled white or brown rice
and steamed snow peas or
cabbage.

1   Place chicken, wine, ginger and garlic
in a bowl and mix to combine. Cover and
set aside to marinate for 30 minutes.
Drain and reserve marinade.

2   Heat oil in a wok or large skillet, add
chicken and stir-fry for 7-10 minutes or
until chicken is almost cooked. Add
reserved marinade, stock and peanut
butter to skillet and bring to the boil.
Reduce heat and simmer for 5 minutes or
until sauce reduces and thickens slightly.
Add spring onions and chili and cook for
1 minute longer. Serve immediately.

Serves 4

STIR-FRY CHICKEN WITH CASHEWS

2 tablespoons vegetable oil
1 red onion, cut into wedges, separated
1 carrot, sliced diagonally
1 clove garlic, crushed
1 teaspoon grated fresh ginger
12 oz/375 g boneless chicken breasts,
cut into strips
1 head broccoli, cut into florets
2 oz/60 g unsalted cashews
$^1/_2$ cup/125 mL chicken stock
2 teaspoons cornstarch
2 teaspoons soy sauce
1 tablespoon dry sherry
$^1/_4$ teaspoon sesame oil
3 spring onions, sliced diagonally

1   Heat 1 tablespoon oil in a wok or large skillet, add onion and carrot and stir-fry for 5 minutes. Add garlic and ginger and cook for 1 minute longer. Remove vegetable mixture from skillet and set aside.

2   Add chicken to skillet and stir-fry for 2-3 minutes or until lightly browned. Remove and set aside.

3   Heat remaining oil in skillet, add broccoli and cashews and stir-fry until broccoli just changes color and cashews are golden.

4   Combine stock, cornstarch, soy sauce, sherry and sesame oil. Return vegetable mixture and chicken to skillet, add cornstarch mixture and cook, stirring constantly, for 3-4 minutes or until sauce boils and thickens. Stir in spring onions and serve immediately.

Serves 4

Stir-frying is one of the most popular methods of Chinese cooking. A wok is best for stir-frying but a large skillet can be used if you do not have a wok. As stir-frying is so quick it is important that you have all your ingredients prepared before you start cooking.

LEFTOVERS

*Turkey is a must for Christmas and
Thanksgiving. But what do you do with the leftovers?
This selection of easy ideas will have you cooking turkey
often, just so you can use the leftovers.*

Turkey Tetrazzini

TURKEY TETRAZZINI

3 oz/90 g plain tagliatelle
3 oz/90 g tomato tagliatelle
3 oz/90 g spinach tagliatelle
$^1/_4$ cup/$^1/_2$ stick/60 g butter
4 slices bacon, chopped
1 onion, chopped
4 oz/125 g mushrooms, sliced
$^1/_3$ cup/45 g all-purpose flour
1$^3/_4$ cups/440 mL chicken stock
$^3/_4$ cup/185 mL heavy cream
2 tablespoons dry sherry
12 oz/375 g cooked turkey, cubed
pinch ground nutmeg
freshly ground black pepper
1 oz/30 g grated Parmesan cheese

Serves 4

1   Cook plain, tomato and spinach tagliatelles together in a large saucepan of boiling water following packet instructions. Drain, set aside and keep warm.

2   Melt butter in a saucepan and cook bacon and onion, stirring, over a medium heat for 4-5 minutes or until onion is soft. Add mushrooms and cook, stirring, for 5 minutes longer or until mushrooms are soft.

3   Stir in flour, then gradually stir in stock and bring to the boil. Reduce heat and simmer, stirring, for 4-5 minutes or until sauce thickens. Remove pan from heat and stir in cream, sherry, turkey, nutmeg, black pepper to taste and tagliatelle.

4   Spoon mixture into an ovenproof dish, sprinkle with Parmesan cheese and bake for 30 minutes or until top is golden.

Oven temperature
350°F, 180°C

When storing leftover turkey, remove the stuffing from the carcass and place in a separate bowl. Cover and refrigerate turkey and stuffing separately.

TURKEY CREOLE

1 tablespoon/15 g butter
1 clove garlic, crushed
1 onion, chopped
1 tablespoon all-purpose flour
1 teaspoon chili powder
$^1/_2$ cup/125 mL tomato juice
$^1/_2$ cup/125 mL chicken stock
12 oz/375 g cooked turkey, chopped
4 oz/125 g button mushrooms, sliced
freshly ground black pepper

Serves 4

1   Heat butter in a saucepan and cook garlic and onion over a medium heat for 3-4 minutes or until onion is soft. Stir in flour and chili powder and cook, stirring, for 1 minute.

2   Stir in tomato juice and stock. Bring to the boil, stirring, over a medium heat, then reduce heat and simmer, stirring, until sauce thickens. Add turkey and mushrooms, season to taste with black pepper, bring to the boil, then reduce heat and simmer for 5 minutes.

Served on a bed of boiled rice, this makes a complete meal that is just right for the day after a feast.

TURKEY NOODLE BAKE

Oven temperature
350°F, 180°C

Remember cooked poultry is best used the next day and should always be used within two days of cooking.

12 oz/375 g egg noodles, cooked
8 oz/250 g cooked turkey, chopped
2 oz/60 g shredded Cheddar cheese
2 stalks celery, chopped
2 cups/500 mL milk
2 eggs
1 teaspoon curry powder
freshly ground black pepper
$^{1}/_{2}$ cup/30 g bread crumbs,
made from stale bread
1 tablespoon/15 g butter

1   Place one-third of noodles in bottom of a lightly greased ovenproof dish. Top with one-third each of turkey, cheese and celery. Repeat layers until all ingredients are used.

2   Place milk, eggs, curry powder and black pepper to taste in a bowl and whisk to combine. Carefully pour milk mixture over ingredients in dish, sprinkle with bread crumbs and dot with butter. Bake for 40 minutes or until firm.

Serves 6

TURKEY HASH

This tasty dish uses those foods that are most often leftover and turns them into something special. If you do not have leftover gravy, use cream of mushroom soup instead.

12 oz/375 g cooked turkey, chopped
2 potatoes, cooked and diced
1 cup/250 mL leftover
turkey gravy
2 spring onions, chopped
freshly ground black pepper
4 slices wholegrain bread, toasted
and lightly buttered
2 tablespoons chopped fresh parsley

1   Place turkey, potatoes, gravy, spring onions and black pepper to taste in a saucepan and bring to the boil, stirring, over a medium heat.

2   Spoon turkey mixture over hot toast, sprinkle with parsley and serve immediately.

Serves 4

Turkey Noodle Bake, Turkey Creole, Quick
Turkey Divan, Turkey Hash

CHICKEN WALDORF MILLEFEUILLE

Oven temperature
425°F, 220°C

6$^1/_2$ oz/200 g prepared puff pastry,
thawed
1 egg, lightly beaten
10 oz/315 g cooked chopped chicken
1 green apple, peeled, cored and
thinly sliced
2 stalks celery, sliced
2 tablespoons golden raisins
3 tablespoons pecans, roughly chopped

BRANDY MAYONNAISE
3 tablespoons mayonnaise
$^1/_2$ cup/125 mL heavy cream
1 tablespoon brandy
pinch ground turmeric
$^1/_2$ teaspoon Dijon mustard
2 teaspoons chopped capers
2 teaspoons snipped fresh chives

1   Roll pastry out to $^1/_8$-inch/3 mm
thickness and cut out six rectangles each
3$^1/_4$ x 5 inches/8 x 12 cm. Place pastry
rectangles on greased cookie sheets, brush
with egg and bake for 10-12 minutes or
until golden.

2   Place chicken, apple, celery, golden
raisins and pecans in a bowl and mix to
combine.

3   To make mayonnaise, place
mayonnaise, cream, brandy, turmeric,
mustard, capers and chives in a bowl and
mix to combine. Spoon mayonnaise over
chicken mixture and toss to coat.

4   To assemble, slit pastry rectangles
horizontally. Place a pastry rectangle on
four individual serving plates, top with
half the chicken mixture, then another
pastry layer. Repeat with remaining
chicken mixture and pastry layers.
Refrigerate until required.

Serves 4

Chicken Waldorf Millefeuille

QUICK TURKEY DIVAN

4 slices bread, toasted and
lightly buttered
8 slices cooked turkey
12 oz/375 g canned asparagus
spears, drained
1 cup/250 mL cream of
asparagus soup
1 cup/250 mL evaporated milk
freshly ground black pepper
3 tablespoons grated fresh Parmesan
cheese

1   Place toast in bottom of a lightly greased, shallow ovenproof dish. Top with turkey slices and asparagus spears.

2   Place soup, milk and black pepper to taste in a bowl and mix to combine. Carefully pour soup mixture over ingredients in dish, sprinkle with Parmesan cheese and bake for 20-25 minutes or until top is golden and mixture bubbling.

Serves 4

Oven temperature
400°F, 200°C

TURKEY AND FETA SALAD

1 pound/500 g cooked turkey, cut into
bite-sized pieces
2 stalks celery, chopped
1 cucumber, peeled, seeded and chopped
12 black olives, pitted
8 oz/250 g feta cheese
1 bunch chicory (curly endive)
1 small bunch watercress

BASIL VINAIGRETTE
1 clove garlic, crushed
4 tablespoons chopped fresh basil
2 tablespoons wholegrain mustard
freshly ground black pepper
1/4 cup/60 mL fresh lemon juice
1/4 cup/60 mL red wine vinegar
1/4 cup/60 mL vegetable oil
1/4 cup/60 mL olive oil

1   To make vinaigrette, place garlic, basil, mustard, black pepper to taste, lemon juice, vinegar and vegetable and olive oils in a screwtop jar and shake well to combine.

2   Place turkey, celery, cucumber, olives and feta cheese in a bowl. Pour over vinaigrette and toss to combine.

3   Arrange chicory (curly endive) leaves on four individual plates, top with salad and garnish with watercress. Serve immediately.

Serves 6 as a light meal

Serve this delicious one-dish salad with crusty rolls or bread for a complete meal.

FRENCH ROAST CHICKEN

1 x 3 pound/1.5 kg chicken
1 cup/250 mL dry white wine
1 cup/250 mL chicken stock
2 tablespoons/30 g butter

CHEESE STUFFING
3 oz/90 g ricotta cheese
2 tablespoons chopped fresh parsley
2 teaspoons chopped fresh tarragon or
$1/2$ teaspoon dried tarragon leaves
4 spring onions, finely chopped
2 tablespoons/30 g butter, softened
freshly ground black pepper

HERB STUFFING
$1/4$ cup/$1/2$ stick/60 g butter
1 small onion, finely chopped
2 stalks celery, finely chopped
2 teaspoons chopped fresh tarragon or
$1/2$ teaspoon dried tarragon
2 tablespoons chopped fresh parsley

1 teaspoon finely grated lemon rind
2 cups/125 g bread crumbs, made
from stale bread
freshly ground black pepper

GRAVY
$1^1/2$ cups/375 mL cooking liquid and
chicken stock
1 tablespoon cornstarch
$1/2$ cup/125 mL heavy cream
freshly ground black pepper

French Roast Chicken

1 To make Cheese Stuffing, place ricotta cheese, parsley, tarragon, spring onions, butter and black pepper to taste in a bowl and mix to combine.

2 Using your fingers, loosen skin on breast of chicken. Push Cheese Stuffing gently under skin, smoothing out evenly.

3 To make Herb Stuffing, melt butter in a saucepan and cook onion for 4-5 minutes or until soft. Place celery, tarragon, parsley, lemon rind and bread crumbs in a bowl, add onion mixture and mix to combine. Season to taste with black pepper. Spoon stuffing into cavity of chicken and secure neck end with metal or bamboo skewers.

4 Truss chicken and place breast side up on a wire rack set in a baking dish. Place wine, stock and butter in dish and bake chicken, turning and basting several times, for 1 hour or until skin is crisp and golden, and chicken is cooked. For the last 15 minutes of cooking, turn the chicken breast side up – this ensures that skin on the breast is crisp. Place chicken on a serving platter and set aside to rest in a warm place for 10 minutes before carving.

5 To make gravy, measure liquid in baking dish and, if necessary, make up to 1^1/2 cups/375 mL with chicken stock. Return liquid to baking dish. Place dish on stove (cooker) top and bring to the boil over a medium heat. Place cornstarch in a small bowl and whisk in cream. Whisk a little hot liquid into the cream mixture, then stir into baking dish. Cook, stirring constantly, for 3-4 minutes or until gravy boils and thickens. Season with black pepper. Serve gravy with chicken.

Serves 4

Paul E. Elson/IMAGE BANK

There should always be liquid in the bottom of the baking dish when roasting the chicken. If the liquid evaporates during cooking, add a little more wine or stock.

Paul E. Elson/IMAGE BANK

You might like to use blue cheese, cream cheese or Camembert in place of the ricotta cheese. If using Camembert, remove rind first.

TRUSSING A CHICKEN

Trussing a chicken helps it maintain its shape during cooking. Insert a metal skewer widthwise, just below the thigh bone, right through the body of the chicken. The ends of the skewer should be exposed either side. Place the chicken breast side down on a work surface. Take a length of string and catch in wing tips, then pass string under ends of skewer and cross over the back. Turn the chicken breast side up and tie in legs and the parson's nose.

CHICKEN WITH SPINACH FILLING

4 chicken marylands (uncut leg
and thigh joints)
2 tablespoons/30 g butter, melted

SPINACH FILLING
4 oz/125 g frozen spinach, thawed
1 clove garlic, crushed
4 oz/125 g ricotta or cottage
cheese, drained
2 teaspoons grated Parmesan cheese
1 teaspoon finely grated lemon rind
pinch ground nutmeg

TOMATO SAUCE
10 oz/315 g canned tomato purée
2 teaspoons Worcestershire sauce

Chicken with Spinach Filling

96

1   To make filling, squeeze spinach to remove excess liquid. Place spinach, garlic, ricotta or cottage cheese, Parmesan cheese, lemon rind and nutmeg in a bowl and mix to combine.

2   Using your fingers, loosen skin on chicken, starting at thigh end.

3   Push filling gently under skin down into the drumstick. Arrange chicken pieces in an ovenproof dish, brush with melted butter and bake for 35-40 minutes.

4   To make sauce, place tomato purée and Worcestershire sauce in a saucepan, bring to simmering and simmer for 3-4 minutes. Serve sauce with chicken.

Serves 4

Drumsticks can be used in place of the chicken marylands if you wish.

Frozen chicken should be completely thawed before cooking. Thaw birds in refrigerator for 24-36 hours or in microwave on DEFROST (30%) for 10-15 minutes per 1 pound/500 g of chicken. Rinse cavity of chicken under cold running water to ensure that there are no remaining ice crystals.

SPICY CHICKEN PIES

Oven temperature
375°F, 190°C

PASTRY
3 cups/375 g all-purpose flour
1/3 cup/90 g butter, cut into pieces
3 oz/90 g lard, cut into pieces
1/3 cup/90 mL cold water
1 egg, beaten

SPICY CHICKEN FILLING
2 tablespoons/30 g butter
2 oz/60 g button mushrooms, chopped
1 onion, chopped
2 teaspoons garam masala
1/4 cup/30 g all-purpose flour
3/4 cup/185 mL chicken stock
10 oz/315 g cooked chicken, diced
2 oz/60 g sweet corn kernels
freshly ground black pepper

1   To make filling, melt butter in a saucepan and cook mushrooms, onion and garam masala over a medium heat for 3-4 minutes or until onion is soft. Stir in flour and cook for 1 minute longer. Add stock and bring to the boil, stirring constantly. Reduce heat and simmer, stirring, for 2 minutes. Remove pan from heat, stir in chicken and sweet corn, season to taste with black pepper and set aside to cool completely.

2   To make pastry, place flour, butter and lard in a food processor and process until mixture resembles fine bread crumbs. With machine running, add water and process to form a firm dough. Turn dough onto a lightly floured surface and knead until smooth.

3   Take two-thirds of the dough and cut into four portions. Roll out each portion to fit a 5-inch/12.5 cm loose-based, fluted tart pan. Line tart pans with pastry, press pastry into flutes, but do not trim top edge. Cut remaining pastry into four portions and roll out each portion to make a lid for each pie.

4   Spoon cold filling into tart pans. Dampen edges of pastry in pans and cover with pastry lids. Using a flat-bladed knife, press edges together to seal and cut off excess pastry. Gather together pastry trimmings, re-roll, then cut out pastry leaves and use to decorate tops of pies. Brush tops with beaten egg.

5   Place pies on a baking tray and bake for 40-45 minutes or until pastry is golden. Remove pies from oven and set aside to cool. When cool, remove from tart pans.

Serves 4

These pies are a delicious picnic food served with a fruit chutney and a crisp salad.

'Delicious as picnic fare or in a packed lunch, you will want to keep a supply of these pies in your freezer.'

PERFECT ROAST TURKEY

Oven temperature
350°F, 180°C

1 x 8 pound/4 kg turkey
$^1/_4$ cup/$^1/_2$ stick/60 g butter, melted
1 cup/250 mL chicken stock

VEAL FORCEMEAT
2 tablespoons/30 g butter
1 onion, finely chopped
1 slice bacon, finely chopped
8 oz/250 g lean ground veal
3 cups/185 g bread crumbs, made
from stale bread
$^1/_2$ teaspoon finely grated lemon rind
$^1/_2$ teaspoon finely chopped fresh parsley
$^1/_2$ teaspoon dried sage
pinch ground nutmeg
1 egg, lightly beaten
freshly ground black pepper

CHESTNUT STUFFING
14 oz/440 g canned chestnut purée,
sieved
2 cooking apples, cored, peeled
and shredded
3 cups/185 g bread crumbs,
made from stale bread
1 onion, finely chopped
1 stalk celery, finely chopped
tablespoons finely chopped walnuts
1 tablespoon finely chopped
fresh parsley
3 tablespoons/45 g butter, melted
1 egg, lightly beaten
pinch ground nutmeg
freshly ground black pepper

Perfect Roast Turkey

1   To make forcemeat, melt butter in a skillet and cook onion and bacon for 4-5 minutes or until bacon is crisp. Add ground veal, bread crumbs, lemon rind, parsley, sage, nutmeg, egg and black pepper to taste. Mix well to combine.

2   To make stuffing, place chestnut purée, apples, bread crumbs, onion, celery, walnuts, parsley, butter, egg, nutmeg and black pepper to taste in a bowl and mix to combine.

3   Remove giblets and neck from turkey. Wipe turkey inside and out and dry well. Place stuffing in body cavity and lightly fill neck end of turkey with forcemeat. Secure openings with metal or bamboo skewers. Tuck wings under body of turkey and tie legs together.

4   Place turkey on a roasting rack in a baking dish. Brush with butter, then pour chicken stock into baking dish. Bake for 3-3$^{1}/_{2}$ hours or until tender. Baste frequently with pan juices during cooking. Set aside in a warm place to stand for 20 minutes before carving.

Serves 10

It is safest to defrost a frozen turkey in the refrigerator for 36-48 hours. Actual defrosting time will of course depend on the size of the bird. Once defrosted, wash bird and rinse out cavity, then pat dry using paper towels. Make sure that there are no ice crystals left in the cavity.

'Cooks have developed many wonderful turkey dishes for special occasions with delicious stuffings and accompaniments. Try this Roast Turkey for a Christmas or Thanksgiving dinner.'

CARVING THE TURKEY

*A very sharp, pointed knife with a long flexible blade is best for carving turkey.
Before you start carving, remove string and skewers from bird and place breast
side up on a board or platter. Use a large carving fork to hold bird steady.*

1 Removing first leg: Cut skin between thigh and breast of bird. Separate leg from body by bending thigh outwards to locate hip joint. Slice down through joint to remove the leg.

2 Separating thigh from drumstick: Hold knife at an angle between thigh and drumstick bones and cut firmly through joint to separate leg.

3 Slicing drumstick: Cut a thick slice of meat and skin from each side of drumstick, keeping knife close to the bone, then cut these into smaller slices.

4 Slicing thigh: Holding thigh steady, cut into four or more pieces, depending on the size of thigh. Repeat steps 1-4 for other leg of turkey.

5 Removing wing: Slice down through corner of breast towards wing. Push wing out to show joint and cut through joint. Remove wing with piece of breast attached.

6 Carving breast: Holding breast steady, slice down through meat. When you reach incision above the wing joint, the slice will fall free.

COOKING TIMES FOR A STUFFED TURKEY

Cook turkeys at 350°F/180°C. If cooked in a hotter oven the outside of the bird browns and cooks before the centre.

Weight	Time
5-6 pounds/2.5-3 kg	2^1/2-3 hours
6-8 pounds/3-4 kg	3-3^1/2 hours
8-12 pounds/4-6 kg	3^1/2-4 hours

CHICKEN STOCK

4 whole cloves
2 onions, halved crosswise
1 chicken carcass, skin removed and
trimmed of all visible fat
12 cups/3 litres cold water
2 carrots, roughly chopped
4 stalks celery, roughly chopped
fresh herbs of your choice
$^1/_2$ teaspoon black peppercorns

1 Stick cloves into onion halves.

2 Place chicken carcass, water, carrots, celery, herbs, peppercorns and clove-studded onions in a large saucepan. Bring to the boil, reduce heat and simmer, stirring occasionally, for 2 hours.

3 Strain stock and refrigerate overnight. Skim fat from surface of stock and use as required.

Makes 8 cups/2 litres

The microwave is particularly good for making small quantities of stock. To make stock in the microwave, place chicken carcass remaining after a roast or raw carcass, 1 chopped onion, 1 chopped carrot, 2 stalks chopped celery, parsley and thyme in a large microwave-safe container. Add water to cover ingredients. Cook, uncovered, on HIGH (100%) for 45 minutes. Strain stock and refrigerate overnight. Skim fat from the surface and use as required.

*'Chicken stock is the basis of many classic dishes.
Stock will keep in the refrigerator for 3-4 days, or in the freezer
for 12 months. Freeze stock in $^1/_2$ cup/125 mL or
1 cup/250 mL portions for easy use at a later date.'*

CRUSTY CHICKEN GOULASH

2 tablespoons vegetable oil
2 large onions, chopped
1¹/₂ tablespoons paprika
2 tablespoons seasoned flour
1 pound/500 g boneless chicken breasts,
cut into strips
1 tablespoon tomato paste (purée)
¹/₂ cup/125 mL red wine
¹/₂ cup/125 mL chicken stock
3 tablespoons plain yogurt

SOUR CREAM CRUST
¹/₂ cup/1 stick/125 g butter, softened
1¹/₄ cups/300 g sour cream
1 egg
1 cup/125 g self-rising flour, sifted
1 tablespoon chopped fresh parsley

Crusty Chicken Goulash

1   Heat 1 tablespoon oil in a large skillet and cook onions, stirring, over a medium heat for 5-6 minutes or until golden. Remove onions from skillet and set aside. Combine paprika and flour in a plastic food bag, add chicken, shake to coat with flour mixture, then shake off excess flour mixture.

2   Heat remaining oil in skillet and cook chicken, stirring, over a medium heat for 2-3 minutes. Return onions to skillet, stir in tomato paste (purée), wine and stock. Bring to the boil, stirring constantly, then reduce heat, cover and simmer for 6-7 minutes. Remove skillet from heat, stir in yogurt and set aside to cool.

3   To make crust, place butter, sour cream and egg in a bowl. Stir in flour and parsley and mix well to combine.

4   To assemble, place crust mixture in an 8 cup/2 litre lightly greased casserole dish and work mixture to cover sides and bottom of dish.

5   Spoon filling into crust, cover with lid of dish and bake for 35 minutes. Remove lid and bake for 10 minutes longer.

Serves 4

Serve this delicious chicken with a tossed green salad or a boiled, steamed or microwaved green vegetable such as green beans, zucchini, snow peas or asparagus.

*'A chicken goulash surrounded by a rich sour cream crust is
just the thing for that special occasion.'*

CHICKEN LIVER PATE

$^1/_4$ cup/$^1/_2$ stick/60 g butter
1 onion, finely chopped
1 clove garlic, crushed
8 oz/250 g chicken livers, chopped
1-2 teaspoons curry powder
$^1/_2$ cup/125 mL chicken stock
2 hard-boiled eggs, cut
into wedges
freshly ground black pepper
cayenne pepper
fresh bay leaves
lemon slices

Chicken Liver Pâté

1 Melt 2 tablespoons/30 g butter in a skillet and cook onion, garlic and chicken livers, stirring, over a medium heat for 5 minutes. Add curry powder and cook for 1 minute longer. Add stock and cook, stirring, for 5 minutes. Remove skillet from heat and set aside to cool for 10 minutes.

2 Place chicken liver mixture and eggs in a food processor or blender and blend to form a smooth purée.

3 Season to taste with black and cayenne peppers. Spoon pâté into a terrine and smooth surface. Melt remaining butter and pour over pâté. Decorate with bay leaves and lemon slices. Refrigerate for several hours. Serve with biscuits or crusty bread.

MICROWAVING POULTRY

As poultry has a low fat content it does not brown naturally when cooked in the microwave, so use a baste or browning agent to add color and flavor.

The following hints will ensure your microwaved birds are perfect:

🍂 Before cooking, tuck wings under bird and tie legs together using a rubber band or string. (Rubber bands do not melt if you use them in the microwave.)

🍂 Start cooking bird, breast side down and turn over halfway through cooking.

🍂 If you wish your bird to have a roasted appearance and taste do not cover during cooking, as covering causes the bird to steam. Cooking a bird in a covered casserole is the ideal way to cook it if you wish to use the flesh in a soup or for chicken salad.

🍂 A stuffed bird will take a little longer to cook. Add 2 minutes to the total cooking time.

🍂 Cook birds elevated on a roasting rack.

🍂 For larger birds, such as turkeys, you may need to shield the wings and drumsticks with aluminum foil during cooking.

🍂 On completion of cooking, cover bird with aluminum foil and allow to stand for 10-15 minutes.

Poultry does not brown naturally during cooking in the microwave so you might like to add color and flavor using one of the following bastes:

🍂 Combine $1/2$ cup/125 mL ketchup, $1/4$ cup/60 mL soy sauce and $1/2$ teaspoon ground ginger. Brush bird with mixture before cooking. Repeat once or twice during cooking.

🍂 Before cooking, brush bird with melted butter, then sprinkle with paprika.

🍂 Combine 2 tablespoons soy sauce, 2 tablespoons sherry and 1 teaspoon finely grated fresh ginger and brush over bird before cooking. Baste once or twice during cooking.

Chicken cooks quickly in the microwave and is moist and tender.

MICROWAVE COOKING CHART

FOOD	POWER LEVEL	COOKING TIMES per 1 pound/500 g
Whole chicken	HIGH (100%)	10 minutes
Chicken pieces	HIGH (100%)	10 minutes
Turkey	HIGH (100%)	10 minutes, then
	MEDIUM-HIGH (70%)	10 minutes
Quail	HIGH (100%)	8 minutes
Duck	HIGH (100%)	10 minutes
Goose	MEDIUM-HIGH (70%)	12 minutes

CHICKEN

What distinguishes a Rock Cornish hen from a chicken? Read on and find out the differences between the various types of birds and what to look for when buying. As part of an everyday diet, chicken is a delicious and healthy food. Most of its fat lies just under the skin, which is easily removed for low-fat cooking.

Whether it's a simple family meal or a formal dinner party, chicken has a place. In recent years its increased availability and moderate price has taken it from being a luxury food to one that can be included regularly as part of your diet.

BUYING: Whole chickens are available fresh or frozen, in a variety of sizes. When buying fresh chicken the bird should have a fresh smell; an unbroken skin with no dark patches; the breast should be plump; the tip of the breastbone soft and pliable; and there should be little moisture on the bird.

Chicken is also sold in pieces – the breast being the most tender and the leanest. Breast chicken is frequently sold as boneless breasts which are suitable for poaching, baking, broiling and pan-cooking. The dark meat on the thighs and drumsticks is higher in fat. The uncut thigh and drumstick portion is called a chicken maryland and is popular crumbed and baked. The wings in small and average-sized birds have little meat but make great finger food when marinated and broiled, baked or barbecued. They are also often used in soups.

ROCK CORNISH HEN: A Rock Cornish hen, is a very small chicken about 5 weeks old and weighing 1-2 pounds/500 g-1 kg. Usually one bird per serving is allowed. It is very tender with a delicate flavor that makes it particularly suited to roasting, pot roasting, casseroling, broiling and barbecuing.

BROILER-FRYERS: Slightly larger and a little older and larger than a Rock Cornish hen, a broiler-fryer is about 8 weeks old and weighs about 2 pounds/1 kg. One bird serves two people.

FOWL OR STEWING HENS: This is an older hen (often 18 months or older) that has stopped laying. It is tough and needs a moist method of cooking. The best way to cook a fowl or stewing hen is to boil or stew it. The cooking time will be about 3 hours, and vegetables are added towards the end of the cooking.

TURKEY: Turkey is available in many guises. Whole birds vary greatly in size from around 5 pounds/2.5 kg to as large as 30 pounds/13.5 kg. Other cuts, such as turkey buffe – which is the breast with the bone in – rolled breast and boneless breasts are also available and have the advantage of being easier to carve. Turkey hindquarters are also an economic and tasty alternative. Turkey is a nutritious low-fat food; in fact it has half the fat and a third of the cholesterol of domestic chicken.

DUCK: Duck has a similar nutrient content to chicken but has twice as much fat. To remove some of the fat during cooking, duck is often cooked on a rack set in a baking dish.

Farmed duck is available both fresh and frozen and should have creamy-white skin with a plump breast. A duck is a bird that is 2-3 months old, weighing 4-6 pounds/2-3 kg, while a duckling is a smaller, younger duck of 6-8 weeks, weighing 3-4 pounds/1.5-2 kg. Wild duck varies greatly in size, age and taste, and requires a moist method of cooking for best results.

QUAIL: Quail is now widely available and is a popular gourmet food. It has a delicate flesh and care should be taken during cooking to prevent it drying out. The average bird weighs 5 oz/155 g and is delicious roasted, braised, pan-cooked or made into pies and pâtés.

STORAGE: The same basic rules apply to all poultry and game birds.

A fresh bird should be removed from its wrapping and placed on a plate then covered lightly so that air can circulate around it.

If preparing the bird in advance, do not stuff it until just prior to cooking. However, the stuffing and the bird can be prepared in advance and stored separately.

To avoid the possibility of salmonella food poisoning, it is important to completely defrost a frozen bird before cooking. To defrost, leave the frozen bird in its original wrapping and place in the refrigerator for 24 hours or longer, depending on its size. Defrosting can also be done in the microwave using DEFROST (30%) and allowing 10 minutes per 1 pound/500 g.

INDEX